DISCOVERING MY **SCARS**

DISCOVERING MY
SCARS

Learning to Take a Giant Leap Forward, While Taking Two Steps Back

STEPHANIE KOSTOPOULOS

NEW YORK

LONDON • NASHVILLE • MELBOURNE • VANCOUVER

DISCOVERING MY **SCARS**
Learning to Take a Giant Leap Forward,
While Taking Two Steps Back

© 2020 STEPHANIE KOSTOPOULOS

Published in New York, New York, by Morgan James Publishing. Morgan James is a trademark of Morgan James, LLC. www.MorganJamesPublishing.com

ISBN 978-1-64279-517-2 paperback
ISBN 978-1-64279-518-9 eBook
Library of Congress Control Number: 2019935759

Cover Design by:
Rachel Lopez
www.r2cdesign.com

Interior Design by:
Bonnie Bushman
The Whole Caboodle Graphic Design

In an effort to support local communities, raise awareness and funds, Morgan James Publishing donates a percentage of all book sales for the life of each book to Habitat for Humanity Peninsula and Greater Williamsburg.

Get involved today! Visit
www.MorganJamesBuilds.com

Dedication

For my nephews and niece, to whom I'm honored to be your aunt. Never be afraid to share your true feelings and be yourself. I hope you read this story one day and understand the world a little better.

Dedication

Contents

Foreword

There are precious few times in my life when I have met someone as self-aware as my friend Stephanie. Although a decade younger than me, she has taught me the gift of self-awareness. Most people lack the courage for true self-awareness. We hide behind our ideas of who we *think we should be* instead of doing the harder work of figuring out *who we really are*. Even fewer of us have what it takes to delve into *why* we are who we are. We think we are the person the world sees. We trade a journey of self-discovery for one of self-acceptance, as if that's even possible when we don't know who we are or why we are.

But as you will see in these pages, Steph is brave.

Brave enough to discover the meaning behind her scars. Courageous enough to dive in and figure out *why* she needed coping mechanisms, instead of settling for hiding them. Steph is so brave that she didn't give up even when her journey of discovery compelled her to confront repressed hurts and expose herself to the pain of trauma all over again. She didn't give up; she never gives up.

She has always been brave, and now her bravery has compelled her to share a deeply personal story.

Parts of her story were known to me, but others were new. Steph and I became friends when we worked together at Killearn United Methodist Church. She and another colleague came into my office one day and asked if I would consider joining a new small group they were starting. Our church had a Celebrate Recovery program, and this was an opportunity to work the twelve steps of recovery together. I'm an easy yes, especially if it's an opportunity for community or self-discovery, and this was both! We supported each other, step by step, and grew to know and appreciate each other in a new way. We each worked on our hurts, habits, and hang-ups by borrowing courage from the group when our own courage failed. More than once, I felt I was borrowing courage from Stephanie.

Later, even when neither of us worked at the church, we found ways to support and encourage one another. I was proud to cheer her on when she launched *Mother Daughter Projects* with her amazing mom, who I am also fortunate to count as a friend. When Steph said she felt as if a book was writing itself inside her, I knew, without a doubt, that her courage would compel her to complete this work.

And now, she's brave enough to turn it over to you. She's the bravest person I know.

—**Beth Demme**, Co-Host of
"Discovering Our Scars" Podcast

Introduction

"I tell you the truth, if you had faith even as small as a mustard seed, you could say to this mountain, 'Move from here to there,' and it would move. Nothing would be impossible."

Matthew 17:20 (NLT)

For two reasons, this verse has always stood out to me. First, mustard is a seed? Second, if a mustard seed *is* really small, I just need that much faith to be able to move a freakin' mountain?

In high school, my church ran a stewardship campaign about growing the church in different ways. They got the idea across by handing out a packet of mustard seeds to each church member. This was the first time I saw a mustard seed. It was so small and perfectly round. I tried planting it, but it never sprouted. What has stayed with me, though, is that faith as small as that tiny thing is all I need. That's a powerful image.

I have many visible scars, as you will learn during this story. But my journey is not just about what can be seen. My scars tell a deeper truth. This truth took me years to discover with a mustard seed of faith. This book recounts that path and where I am today.

I am now sharing this journey because for twelve years, I have had an overwhelming feeling that I *need* to share this in a public way. I have fought this feeling and put the pages away many times. But the need to share is greater. I now know I went through this trauma and discovery for a reason, and it's important to publicly share my story.

This book is for you—you, who just started reading and have no idea what you're getting into. You, who might have a similar past and can relate. You, who needs to read this story, because it might help you understand someone in your life better. Whoever you are, welcome! My name is Steph. Nice to meet you.

Scars come in all shapes and sizes, and they result from all sorts of trauma. Major themes and subject matter on my journey involve mental illness, psychiatric hospitals, and childhood abuse. These are hard topics to discuss and read about. Please note some names have been changed, but the people are all real. I have done my best to share what is important. Please know I share this to tell my truth fully and honestly.

This journey begins with Part 1, which takes place over a span of four days—a total of seventy-four hours—in a psychiatric system and jumps backward in time to see how I got to the present. Part 2 covers the six years after the hospital and explores post-traumatic stress disorder (PTSD) and discovered childhood abuse. Part 3 focuses on Christ-centered recovery, more childhood revelations, and where I am today.

If you or someone you know is struggling with mental illness, you are not alone. I hope my story may encourage your own recovery. Now, on with the show…

PART 1
Hospital

CHAPTER ONE

12 Hours

The rage grew; I couldn't take having my world turned completely upside down. When I lived with my parents, home was a place of peace and calm. Now, in my college dorm with three random roommates, I couldn't find that anymore—anywhere! I had to call another roommate meeting because AJ had eaten my food again! She disrespected me— again! Her actions made me feel unsafe and unsettled in my own home.

Our hall resident advisor was in attendance, again, to mediate between me, Megan, and AJ; my other roommate, DeeDee, was at church. Megan was always on my side, mainly there to support me. But as the meeting progressed, nothing changed. AJ still didn't care and showed through her body language that she thought my "concerns" were not valid and not worth her time. She had come to the University of Central Florida (UCF) from Russia, so I couldn't tell whether it was a cultural thing or an attitude problem.

The conversation was going nowhere, and I couldn't take it anymore! I left the meeting in the dorm kitchen and stormed off to my room. I wanted to punch someone or something. Adrenaline raced through my blood, and my brain had shut itself off to reason. I turned to my old coping method when emotions got too much to handle. Life was catching up with me, and it was time to set it free! I did not release my anger with a hit. I released it with a cut ... seven slashes with scissors, horizontally from my left wrist to the inside of my left forearm. My flesh was covered in red.

Then, my racing mind calmed. My eyes slowly closed. I took a calming breath. I could now identify the location and cause of my pain.

Seconds later, as the haze lifted from my eyes, reality set in and I saw only red. I screamed for Megan. She entered the room, looked at me for a split second, and dialed 911. Our resident advisor came in to help me wrap up my arm to stop the bleeding. She told me not to look, so I didn't. AJ came in for a second, looked disgusted, and left.

Shortly afterward, the paramedics arrived. Still, I didn't look at the open wound. I felt no pain. My brain was in a fog. There was so much to process that I couldn't process any of it. I was just a shell of a person, unable to connect my body, brain, and heart with the reality of the situation. The paramedics told me it was not that bad and I didn't need stitches. I nodded, hearing the words but connecting to nothing.

What's going on? Why are the paramedics here? Why are so many people in my bedroom? Where's my mom? These questions swirled in my head as I looked around, unable to get a grip on reality.

The paramedics wrapped my forearm with gauze and left. Each moment was moving too fast. I didn't feel like the girl in the room; I felt like I was watching the scene from a camera high up. I watched my mouth move and words come out when I was spoken to. But I didn't choose the words. They were an auto-response based on each question.

Next, Police Officer Eddie Moen came to my dorm room and sat on the floor next to me. He looked like a big kid in a police uniform. He didn't ask much about what happened, but he did ask to see the wound. As he examined it, his face didn't flinch. Then he covered my arm back up and told me he wanted to take me to a place that could help. My brain was spinning as it tried to catch up with what was going on.

"Can I take you there?" he asked.

Take me where? I thought. All I knew was my world had just exploded and my arm was badly cut. I didn't know where he wanted to take me or what they would do for me, but I assumed they would help with my arm. My automatic response to his question: "Yes." I was wearing shorts and a T-shirt. I put on flip-flops, grabbed my purse, and got into the police car.

UCF dorm room: bottom, second from left

Riding in the backseat felt odd. Up to that point, I had no experience with the police. Never been arrested, never pulled over—nothing. And there I was, riding through campus in the back of that car with the once-familiar buildings and athletic fields looking unworldly from that foreign vantage point. It was Sunday, October 8, 2006, around 4:30 in the afternoon. We got on the interstate and Moen just kept driving. I had recently moved to Orlando, Florida, so I had no idea where we were going.

• • • • •

The police car slowed. The only sound—a short screech of tires. I guess we had arrived. It was still light outside, but I couldn't identify anything around me. We parked under an awning like they have at hotels, where the bellhops help bring in your stuff. But no one came to help.

The run-down medical-looking building now facing me was no hotel I wanted to stay in. It looked like it could be a hospital, so I figured it was a place to fix my arm. Everything seemed eerie; no one else was around and there were no cars in the parking lot. The place almost looked abandoned. I wasn't sure if I was about to walk into Disney's Tower of Terror ride or a hospital.

Officer Moen opened the car door and escorted me inside. I stood quietly as he talked to the man behind the office desk. Moen then left with a quick goodbye, and the staff person asked for my belongings.

I sat quietly as he took everything out of my purse and listed all the contents on a form. While he did this, he directed me to a bathroom and told me to put on blue paper scrubs and to pee in a cup. He put my purse and clothes into a plastic bag and wrote my name on it. He asked me no questions about what happened in my dorm room; he just had me sign countless forms with the name "Central Receiving Center" (CRC) on them. Knowing the name still didn't help me know where I was or what would happen to me. He asked about my insurance; I told him it was in my wallet.

After all that, he sent me to the waiting room—leaving me with nothing to do and no idea where I was. I sat quietly, my arm tightly wrapped, my mind a blank. I was still a shell and didn't know what was going on or how I had even gotten to this point. The TV set was on, and my eyes just stared at the moving pictures.

Eventually, the nurse called me in for my medical exam and escorted me into a tiny room with a few supplies. It looked like a large closet. The nurse took my bandage off, all the while not saying anything to me or making eye contact. She looked at my arm in disgust for a few moments, then she exclaimed with an attitude, "What is this? Look at this!"

That took me aback. She hadn't said two words to me and when she did, they were intense. Reluctantly, I looked at my uncovered arm. I wasn't ready for the sight. It was still bright red, with a mix of dried and fresh blood. I couldn't even make out the cut marks, there was so much blood. As the nurse stood waiting for me to take it all in, all I could do was cry. The physical pain was overwhelming, with the bloody wound exposed to air. But the emotional pain of being forced to take it all in so soon afterward was indescribable.

"Who did this?" she said in a knowing tone. "Why are you crying? *You* did this!"

As I continued to sob, she said, "You did this to yourself. You don't get to cry over this!"

A kaleidoscope of emotions crashed inside of me. The shell of my body and brain were trying desperately to connect to my heart, but the nurse wouldn't allow me to express my emotions fully, so I just went numb. I maintained that empty shell, disconnected and observing myself from above. I stopped crying and did what I was told.

The nurse looked at my arm again with disgust and put the bandage back on. "This looks like raw hamburger meat. I can't do anything with this. You have to go to the ER," she spat.

Just like that, I was back in the waiting room with no more instructions. I replayed the nurse's words in my head: *raw hamburger meat.* That graphic description of my arm struck me hard. And with one look, she had said I needed to go to the ER.

Why did the UCF paramedics say I was fine? Why didn't they send me to the ER? I was lost and confused.

After waiting for hours, reality hit. I asked if I could call my dad. Along with being my dad, he is also a doctor—a doctor of philosophy in psychology. When I tell people my dad is a psychologist, most imagine that he is a counseling psychologist, where patients sit on a couch and tell him their problems.

Well, that's not my dad. He exclusively administers and interprets clinical testing. He works at a mental hospital in my hometown of Tallahassee, Florida. When patients are admitted, he tests them to see what mental illnesses they might have so the psychiatrist can better diagnose and prepare a treatment plan.

I called my dad because I thought he might have some insight about what I should do and what was going to happen. On the phone, I told him through tears what had occurred. He told me to follow the process and that I would be okay. At the time, his words comforted me.

Hours went by as I sat with nothing to do. I started replaying the day's events.

This morning, I was at the sorority house, learning who my big sister was. Wow, that was stressful; I had never met her before. But I did it and got through the sorority ritual. Then I headed to my dorm around 4 p.m. for a few minutes to grab food because I hadn't eaten all day. When I got home, I found my food gone—eaten again by AJ. That's when I lost it. I was probably more charged than usual because I was hungry and don't do well without fuel.

Months prior, I had created a healthy eating plan for myself and had all my meals planned out and ready for the week. I was overweight as a child, so I wanted to take control of my health and not gain the stereotypical freshmen fifteen … and now, I had ended up here. I still didn't know where *here* was or what they would do for/to me. Did I really end up here because my roommate ate my food?

• • • • •

A little before 11 p.m., a minibus pulled up at CRC. After a twenty-minute drive in the bus, we arrived at the ER and a female handler escorted me inside. I still had on the blue paper scrubs, with a blanket around me, and the handler was holding my belongings bag. We waited at the front desk with all eyes on me. What a sight I must have been! The man at the desk asked my handler what treatment I needed; she didn't know and looked to me for answers. I had no answers, so they just admitted me. My handler left, and the man sat me in a chair behind the counter.

He made me show my wound to several ER workers for their opinion about whether I needed stitches. Everyone reacted the same: cringing, looking at my face with disgust or horror, shaking their heads. No one asked me what happened. No one asked me how I felt. No one asked me if I was okay.

But everyone agreed that I needed stitches.

By now, nearly seven hours had passed since the event in my dorm. It frustrated me that the UCF paramedics had only wrapped my arm and said it was fine. I still wonder how much better my scars would have healed if I had been sent to the ER right after the event happened.

About an hour later, a staffer took me to a room to be stitched up. At twenty, I had never been to a hospital, never had a broken bone—not even a tooth cavity. I didn't know what to expect and what stitches would feel like. This was a scary place to be in for the first time—especially without my mom to hold my hand.

In the procedure room, the doctor numbed my arm. It felt like a million tiny pins were being stuck into my open wound, but I guess that was better than feeling him put the stitches in. Even with my arm numbed, I could feel the tugging and pulling from the needle. It felt like someone was sewing my skin. I could feel the extra material as it lay next to my skin before it became a stitch. Then it was over—twenty-four stitches in all.

They set up a rolling bed for me in the hallway. Finally, at 12:45 a.m., I ate for the first time that day (well, I guess it was technically Monday at that point). A nurse had brought me a turkey sandwich, and the food definitely helped. After eating, I tried to sleep, but staff and other patients kept interrupting me.

First, an intern woke me and put Vaseline on my arm and wrapped it. Other patients were talking, and some yelled in pain from their own hallway beds. The faces of those who looked after me showed no compassion. I guess they didn't feel the need to show me any because they felt, as they kept reminding me, "you did this to yourself." I did sleep a little bit, but I woke up from the constant noise. My eyes opened, and according to the clock, it was three in the morning.

I was hopeful I would leave soon, so I went to the bathroom to freshen up. This was the first time I had seen my reflection in eleven hours. I saw a girl who had been up almost twenty-four hours, been through more real drama than high school, and had cried freely for what felt like days. Her dignity, respect, and sanity had been stripped away.

I had never seen myself like this before. I had been a shell of a person for so many hours, just watching myself from above. But now I was face to face with reality. I didn't recognize this girl with the deep-black bags under her puffy eyes, almost hiding the dark-brown eyes within. Her lips were drained of any color, and her full face was a pale shade of gray … as if I only saw in black and gray now. And her expression—emotionless. But in that, I could still see the deep pain, fear, and lost girl within.

Is this my true reflection or the reflection of how the world has torn me down? Is this all my doing? Why have I coped with self-injury to deal with my emotions for so many years? The image of that girl is still seared in my memory today.

CHAPTER TWO

High School

Where do you begin when you have a lifetime of memories that precede an event? My childhood was filled with two present parents, a brother, and a nice group of friends. We lived in a quiet neighborhood with a big backyard where my brother and I would frequently dig big holes because ... why not! I had a best friend right across the street who I hung out with daily, jumping on her trampoline, playing in her tree fort, or making pretend music in our band with instruments we had made out of cardboard. Most of life was fun, but school was a challenge.

In first grade, my dad and my school diagnosed me with dyslexia, a learning disability. This meant I had to work harder than my friends to learn. I adapted though and didn't let it hold me back. Although I can't remember a lot of my childhood, life seemed pretty good most of the time as an elementary-aged girl.

When I was in middle school and high school, life got harder. My parents took notice and, when I was fourteen, my dad gave me a test for depression. He had given me many psychological tests over the years. It was how he practiced his new children's tests—I was his test subject. The tests were for intelligence, memory, attention, etc. But this was different. The depression test was not for practice. Dad gave it to me to see if I was damaged, to see if I was sick, like his patients.

After Dad scored my test, he delivered the results in his "work voice." Mom was sitting to his left.

Have you ever had a doctor speak down to you? Maybe scold you for not exercising like you should? Maybe make you feel like they have a higher place in the world because they have "Dr." before their name? Well, all that and more is what my dad's "work voice" sounds like. It's very patronizing and even has a little chuckle in it, as if he is saying, "I know so much more than you. Every word that comes out of my mouth has so much more value than what you say."

I might as well call him by his professional name, Dr. Lawrence, because there's no trace of my dad when he talks to me like this.

Alas, the test results weren't good. They showed that I was deeply depressed. I had a mental illness. Then Dr. Lawrence proceeded to go through my answers to the fill-in-the-blank questions and told me the answers he felt were most troubling.

"Why did you write this?" he asked me. "What did you mean by that?" he kept repeating.

"I don't know," I answered. I said that because I really didn't know. I had answered the questions quickly, as he had instructed, and didn't think a lot about them. Yet, now he wanted me to think *why*. At fourteen, I didn't know *why*. I didn't know what was causing me to be depressed, and I didn't understand my overwhelming emotions.

This news upset my parents, so I tried to act happier around them. My emotions scared me; I didn't know how to handle them—so I shut them down. I did my best to ignore them and fill my time with other activities. I must have put on a really good show because, eventually, no one asked if I was depressed anymore. My parents let the depression results drain from their thoughts, and they didn't seek treatment for me.

• • • • •

I joined the Girl Scouts when I was eight years old and loved it. The smell of a roaring fire, s'mores, and dew in the morning always reminds me of Scouts. But freshman year of high school, that fun was about to end. My troop had a falling out, and just two of us were left.

I couldn't say goodbye to the campouts, service projects, and being silly with my friends yet. So, I did

some recruiting! I planned a sleepover and invited some of my new high school friends. I didn't tell them what I was planning; I just invited them over for some fun. Ultimately, out of the ten girls I invited to my recruitment sleepover, five of them wanted to join the troop. So, the troop was back—seven girls strong!

Even though we were in high school, we still had to sell Girl Scout cookies. We found it hard to sell them in front of the grocery store since we weren't cute six-year-olds anymore.

No matter, we decided to sell cookies at our high school. I don't know many people who would be comfortable selling Girl Scout cookies at their school, but my friends were! We sold so many cookies that, after just a few days, we didn't have to sell much more. That's what I loved about my ladies: They were not embarrassed to do out-of-the-box things and have fun with it!

• • • • •

During my sophomore year of high school, 9/11 happened. As bad and unimaginable as it was, my brother had joined the Air Force just weeks before and was in basic training. He called us the night of the attacks, just long enough to say that he was okay. I felt a pain and sadness I had never experienced before. I couldn't wrap my head around so many innocent lives being lost.

I still can't imagine what it must have been like on the streets of New York that day and what people can never unsee. And in my head, behind all that sadness and destruction, was my brother—alone, away from the family, on a military base with little training under his belt.

Questions kept swirling in my fifteen-year-old head. Are the bad guys going to target military bases? Are they coming for my brother next? Does this mean war? Does this mean my brother is going to war?

Shortly after he finished basic training, he was sent to Afghanistan. That was a hard time emotionally for me. The emotions I had shut down so well came roaring back, stronger than ever before. To cope, I journaled a lot and wrote letters to my brother. We wrote things to each other that we would never say in person. I had less fear sharing my deep feelings with him. I guess the fear that I might not ever get to say those things to him was greater than the fear of expressing them.

• • • • •

Most of my high school career was made up of me making videos. I took a TV production class in my sophomore year and knew production was for me. Making videos was a way to share my feelings with the world in a way I couldn't do with words. With video editing, I could craft a story out of nothing.

Early on, my parents saw this passion in me and invested in a professional video camera and iMac computer. They joked that I had never needed braces, so my video equipment was paid for with the money they had set aside for that.

I spent hours behind my camera and editing on my Mac. I never had a computer before that I enjoyed using. Computers were always just tools that I had to use for school. But not my Mac. I fell in love with the process of video editing: capturing files, moving each frame, creating a story, and exporting it for others to see.

I didn't feel depressed when I was working on productions. I felt whole. I felt complete. I didn't know what and I didn't know how, but I knew my life's work would involve production in some way. Video production became my passion.

• • • • •

As high school came to a close, I would see depression in another person for the first time: my Girl Scout friend Megan (who just happens to share the same name as one of my college roommates).

My Volvo was packed with four suitcases for spring break. A safety whistle dangled around each of my friends' necks, and my own—gifts from my mom that we all planned to ditch when we arrived in Orlando. This was my first spring break with no parents, hanging out with my Girl Scout friends for five days at Disney! But after we made the four-hour drive and spent a day at the parks, I saw Megan change.

She became a shell of her former self. She didn't want to talk to us. She didn't want to be around us, and she didn't want anything to do with the fun we were having. I don't mean that she just didn't want to be our friend anymore—it was different. It was not childish, and it was not catty. It was the darkness of depression, although I didn't know it at the time.

We all stayed in a hotel room together and, one night, Megan wanted to go to bed at nine. The rest of us were not ready for bed, but we let her sleep and the three of us gathered in the hallway, sat on the floor, and played cards.

I was upset with Megan for not enjoying our trip. But as the weeks went on, long after we came back home, I continued to see a deep hurt in her. It scared me, probably because deep down I knew I was depressed too. I just hid mine better. I tried to convince Megan to get some therapy, but she wasn't open to it. We stayed friends through the beginning of community college, but then she dropped out. I didn't see her much after that.

When I started cutting and feeling the effects of deep depression, Megan's face would come to my mind. I wanted to reach out to her; I wanted to tell her I understood it now. I wanted to talk to her for help. But I was too lost for that.

Mer, Me, Megan, and Emily by
my Volvo before our Orlando trip

CHAPTER THREE

24 Hours

After getting my stitches and waiting to be picked up, I left the ER around 4 a.m. and was taken back to CRC, where Officer Moen had brought me about twelve hours before. This time, I was told a little bit of information. I needed to finish my nurse evaluation, then I would have my mental assessment. I was complacent because I thought the assessment was the last part. Make a good impression, then I could go home!

Shortly after I arrived back, I was taken to a small room. The woman who came in to assess me looked pretty young and didn't speak English very well. I told her about my struggles with self-injury and the treatment I was seeking with my psychologist, Dr. Jill, in Tallahassee.

I told her that Dr. Jill knew me and my history, and to please call her for details. I told her about the stress of moving to Orlando, into a dorm with strangers, and about AJ, who did not respect my property. I answered her questions clearly and concisely. When we were done, she just left me in the room. *What's next?* I thought.

A few minutes later, a nurse came in and brought me to the back room, which looked like a waiting room at a doctor's office. It had about forty chairs, thirty of them occupied by people. I looked around at the faces and wondered what had brought each person here. It seemed strange to me that Orlando had created a Central Receiving Center for anyone who showed signs of mental illness. The staff did not seem properly trained for our needs.

Having us all crammed into this small room, I thought, was like saying, *These are all animals. Let's put them all in one cage together.* But, we know that wouldn't work because animals need different habitats (and some would eat each other). They all need to be treated in different ways to have successful, healthy lives—especially in captivity.

The nurse told me to sit in the small room until I was transferred somewhere else.

Somewhere else? Does that mean my assessment didn't go well? Do they think I belong in a mental hospital? Is this the mental hospital or is that "somewhere else"? Am I really crazy?... I was lost in my thoughts.

I tried not to make eye contact with anyone else because I wasn't feeling chatty. But I looked across from me and caught the eyes of a large man. His eyes were full of sadness and pain. I looked away, but then he started talking with a Cuban accent.

He told me a little about himself, which I found far better than watching soap operas on TV. He had attempted suicide thirteen times and lived in a mental health facility.

He was a soldier in a war. He saw people blown up in front of him. He blew people up, and he saw his friends killed. He told me about being so hungry in the woods that he cut the throat of a wolf and ate it. He ate it all. Then he threw it up. He acted out the action of cutting the throat. His eyes showed a glimmer of joy when describing the kill, as if it was satisfying. I could see how the anger and trauma he experienced in war was taken out on that wild beast.

He told me of his ex-wife and daughter. He had lost them both due to his hallucinations and hearing the voices of his soldier friends. The voices told him to kill himself. He told me a few ways he had tried to accomplish this goal. His words made me feel sad. War had destroyed his life. My brother killed from the air. This man killed countless men right in front of his face. *What must that do to a person?* I thought, *Well, I guess I'm seeing it right here.*

As he spoke to me, I kept thinking, *I'm too young to hear this. This is really crazy stuff!*

During the conversation, however, I connected with him on a human level and saw the path that brought him here. I knew he needed help, but I feared he would not find it in this system. This conversation changed me; I would never be a twenty-year-old naive sorority girl again.

After waiting for a few hours, I called my dad again. I told him what I knew, which wasn't much. He was in Tallahassee with my mom, and there was little they could do from there. They thought about coming down to help, but Dad told me to do what they said and I would get out quickly. This continued to be his advice each time I called; it was of little comfort. I was already doing what I was told. I was not making a scene, and I was keeping calm as the hours passed.

With all the free time and nothing to do, I called my psychologist, Dr. Jill. I told her what all was going on, and she seemed very concerned. CRC had not called her; this was the first she'd heard of me being in the hospital. She was upset for me and that I was "in the system." I didn't know what the "system" was, but it didn't sound good.

"You should never have been sent there. You are not a danger to yourself. Tell your dad to call down there and get you out!" Dr. Jill exclaimed. This confused me because Dad did not share her concerns. I told her I would try to reach him again.

"They cannot legally keep you longer than twenty-four hours," Dr. Jill assured me. This was *very* encouraging. It was Monday morning, so they would have to release me by at least 5 p.m.

Probably sooner than that, I thought. *Maybe I can even make my 3 p.m. class!*

The next eight hours were a blur. I freaked out a couple of times and called my parents. "Get me out of here. I want to go home!" I yelled this through tears and didn't care about the stares.

During this time, the nurse changed my bandage and "cleaned" my stitches by drowning them with peroxide. That did not feel great. Not great at all. Meanwhile, my 3 p.m. class came and went. As the clock crept closer to 5 p.m., I started getting frantic. I had spent nearly twenty-four hours locked up with nothing to do but sit in my stress, anxiety, and shame.

It was now nearing 6 p.m. on Monday. No one would answer my many questions: "What am I waiting for? Where will I be transferred? How long will I be here? What is the result of my assessment?"

Dr. Jill called me back and said she would talk to my dad about getting me out. She also asked me if I was "Baker Acted or voluntarily came." I didn't know what any of that meant.

She explained that if I had refused to come to the hospital, then I would or could have been Baker Acted if the police officer thought I was a danger to myself or others. This is a Florida legal action, and I would have to be assessed in twenty-four hours. They would have to let me go if they could not find evidence that I was a danger.

I thought it through. *When was I asked about going to a mental hospital? I couldn't remember.*

Then it hit me. Officer Moen said he wanted to take me someplace that would "help." He asked if I was okay with that, and I had said, "Yes." I wanted to do the right thing, and if he thought this place was right, I trusted him. I trusted the police officer like I was brought up to do. He never said it was a mental hospital. He never said I wouldn't be able to leave. He never said my rights and dignity would be stripped away.

So, there it was. I had come voluntarily. Dr. Jill said she was not sure what would happen.

"When the hospital is not legally required to release, they have been known to keep people longer who have good insurance," she told me.

She encouraged me to find a release form to sign so they would have to legally release me.

After hanging up with Dr. Jill, I called my dad to see what I should do. I explained what Dr. Jill said, but he didn't agree.

"They will not keep you longer than they need to. They have plenty of patients they need to see and are not going to keep you for no reason," my dad—I mean, Dr. Lawrence—said.

At that, I yelled and cursed at my dad. I couldn't take this major contradiction from these psychologists anymore.

"Calm down. Get control of yourself!" he said this with force and authority, as if I was his patient and he had lost his calm with me. His actions only made me more unsettled and fearful of the "system" that I found myself in the middle of.

I hung up on Dr. Lawrence and started to pace the tiny space the thirty of us were all jammed into. After a while, I noticed a small room about the size of a closet off to the side. It had white walls and was completely empty. I couldn't figure out its purpose. It seemed to be wasted space. I decided it was a nice, quiet place for me to try to calm down.

I was exhausted after being awake for nearly twenty-four hours since this nightmare began, so I sat on the floor in the dark room—alone and crying. Still wearing the thin blue paper scrubs from the night before, I held my legs close to me and rocked back and forth. Intense anger and frustration accumulated inside me. I had the incredible urge to run, punch, kick, yell, roll over, and fetch a stick—anything! I couldn't just sit and do nothing. Sit. Nothing. Sit. Sit. Sit. Sit. S**t!

"I'm going crazy. This place makes you crazy!" I said out loud to myself.

One kind nurse finally tried to comfort me, but I was long past that point. I was shaking on the floor. I unloaded my thoughts out loud...

"My dad is a nightmare! He's one of them! He doesn't get it! He acts like he's superior to others, because he does, of course, think he is superior to mentally ill people. He thinks there's nothing wrong with the system, that the system doesn't fail, and that there's only good people in the world. Look at my world, Dad! Look at what's right f*** in front of you!"

I paused and tried to take a breath through my full, flowing tears. "Well, at least we have the same political views. I would've given up all hope on him if we didn't," I whispered, as if to still connect to my dad in some simple way.

I thought back to growing up. My parents didn't use curse words, and they didn't allow us to either. I was okay with that; I actually liked it not being part of my vocabulary. Maybe I didn't care about those words because I was never in a situation where I really needed them. But now—freedom, choice, and dignity taken from me—all I had were words. These words flowed out of me like never before.

I soon lost my breath. I couldn't breathe. I had found my crazy place where no light shined in, and voices could not be understood. The nurse left me there. I was all alone, shaking on the floor. I heard no sounds around me. I saw no human beyond me. I was at my lowest, my craziest—and then a memory popped into my head.

At age six, I went to my bedroom, turned off the lights, and asked God to live with me forever. I was prompted to make this commitment after my little ears heard about it in church earlier that day. I didn't really understand it at the time, but I knew God was good and I wanted Him to be part of my life. It was a powerful moment.

As I sat on the cold vinyl floor, the nurse came back in and turned on a bright light. As I looked up at her, squinting at the light, she handed me a card. It had a white dove on the front with a message inside. It was from Matt, a youth pastor from my hometown church who now lived in Orlando.

"Stephanie, hi!" his note said. "I'm a hospital chaplain, so let me know when you get to where you're going and I'll stop by. Matt."

That was the truth of the moment, but the symbolism in the moment was far greater. As I looked up into the bright light, in the midst of desperation, I saw the hand of God reach out to me and a dove fly freely from it. It flew calmly and gracefully, surrounded by bright light. As I watched the dove, I heard God say, "I am here. And there is another human who cares and wants to help, right outside. You can make it through. Stand strong. I am with you."

I stopped shaking and held the tiny card in my hand—this was mine—from another human who cared. This gave me the strength to get through the last hours at CRC.

The simple card Matt gave me,
photo by Daniel Kuykendall

CHAPTER FOUR

Community College

I n middle school, I started taking birth control pills to regulate my hormones because I had really painful periods. But as a middle schooler and then high schooler who was not sexually active, I hated being on the pill. Picking my prescription up from the store embarrassed me.

At age eighteen, when I started Tallahassee Community College, I wanted to be done with the pill. I had taken it for six years and thought my periods wouldn't be so bad anymore. So, I stopped. I didn't think about this much or try to take note of things that might be different. I just enjoyed my life and community college.

But as the days and weeks went by, depression started to set in … harder than ever before. It was slow, but it built into an overwhelming cloud of darkness. Everywhere I went, it followed. It was a heaviness that caused more pain with every step—every breath. I felt so much pain inside but had no physical pain to show for it. I couldn't say, "Look, my arm is broken. This is what hurts."

One day, the mysterious internal pain became so severe that after class, in my bedroom, I cut the inside of my left forearm with scissors. I needed to *see* the pain I felt inside, and for some reason, this is what my brain told me to try. It helped. The sting on my arm was enough to relieve the pain inside. It allowed me to go on playing the part of a normal human in society. I don't know how my brain came up with this way to cope—it just popped up as a thought, and I saw it through to reality.

I continued this ritual when I was depressed or when I just needed to feel something. A lot of anger was associated with my depression too. I would hit the punching bag in my room for about twenty minutes, and then I would cut my arm. Hitting the bag helped get some of the anger and rage out before I took the scissors to my skin. I didn't even want to think about cutting my arm before punching the bag, because if I'd taken all of my pent-up anger out on my arm, I might have seriously hurt myself. I always punched the bag, then cut.

I always cut my arms and always with a pair of orange-handled scissors. This was the only thing that satisfied my pain. No one saw the marks. They faded, or I would cover them up. This was not for others to know, see, or question.

While in health class one day, I read about premenstrual dysphoric disorder (PMDD). It sounded just like me. The Mayo Clinic's website explains it perfectly:

> Premenstrual dysphoric disorder (PMDD) is a severe, sometimes disabling extension of premenstrual syndrome (PMS). Symptoms usually begin seven to 10 days before your period starts and continue for the first few days that you have your period. PMDD has at least one of these emotional and behavioral symptoms stand outs: sadness or hopelessness, anxiety or tension, extreme moodiness, marked irritability or anger. Treatment of PMDD is directed at preventing or minimizing symptoms and may include antidepressants, birth control pills, nutritional supplements, herbal remedies, diet and lifestyle changes.

There it was: Birth control can help. The pill might have been what kept my depression in check during middle and high school. But in community college, when I had nothing to fight the depression, my symptoms were in full swing. At the time, I noted that antidepressants were another possible treatment. That seemed like a great way to get help without having to take birth control pills again.

One day after class, I went to the gym and hopped on a treadmill. I walked on it like others were doing on the treadmills around me. I'm sure I seemed "normal" like them. But inside, I was so depressed. I couldn't think of anything ... except not being alive anymore. I just kept walking in place and thinking about what it would be like to end my life.

As I was drowning in these thoughts, I jumped back into reality and wondered if this meant I was suicidal. I didn't think I was, because every time I had the thoughts, I arrived at the same conclusion: I could never do that to my family and friends. It would be so unfair to take my life, which would in turn really hurt the people I love, especially because they did not know I was experiencing such pain.

That's when I made a decision: I would know I was suicidal and in need of help when I felt the need to write a suicide note. I could not kill myself without explaining why to my family and friends. I would not go through with anything without that simple act.

Through my life, I have been lower than low—I have spent days just wishing I was no longer on the planet—but I never wrote that note. I came close, but I could never do it—not for the love of myself in those moments, but for the love of my family.

● ● ● ● ●

While driving to class one day, the song "What Are You Waiting For" played on the radio and really spoke to me. It was the summer of 2006, and I was about to graduate community college with my Associate of Arts degree and move on to UCF and major in television production.

The reality set in that I could not move on from everything I had ever known with my secret cutting life. I knew I would not make it on my own. I had to tell my mom. I knew she would be supportive and get me help. But to tell her about my secret world of depression and coping—that would be the hardest thing I ever had to do.

I stopped at Target before class to buy the Natalie Grant album that the song I'd just heard on the radio was featured on. I listened to every song, which calmed me and gave me the courage to talk to Mom. I was just two months away from moving to Orlando.

A few days later, I was sitting in the passenger seat, a little warm because it was summertime and Mom had turned the car off. We just sat. We were waiting for our usual Sunday after-church restaurant to open. Then I got even hotter, because I knew this was the moment.

"Mom, I have something to tell you," I said. I told her that I was depressed, had been cutting my arm, and wanted to get help. She sighed in relief and said, "Is that it? Well, we'll get you help this week."

Mom scheduled an appointment with my primary care doctor, who prescribed me Zoloft for the depression. Then my parents found a psychologist, and I started seeing her for counseling within a week.

Before my first counseling session, I didn't know what to expect. I wondered if there would be a couch I would have to lie on and if the doctor would ask me "How do you feel about that?" All my therapy references came from TV shows, and the shows never really got into how the healing happens.

Dr. Jill's office was on the second floor of a law firm, so when I checked in at the desk, someone directed me to the stairs. I walked in and saw a couch with an armchair right across from it. Dr. Jill welcomed me and invited me to sit on the couch.

From the very first session, therapy went really well. It was freeing to have dedicated time to talk to a psychologist and not feel judged. I told her about the cutting and the feelings I couldn't explain. She listened closely to me, asked questions, and took it all in.

Dr. Jill told me that I'm not a "cutter" and not suicidal. My "cutting," she said, was classic self-injury. I injured myself to *feel*, not to end my life. This news brought me huge relief. I didn't think I wanted to kill myself, but I was scared and didn't understand the complexities and differences in mental illness.

She agreed that the selective serotonin reuptake inhibitor (SSRI) medication should help with my depression. I could tell she didn't think self-injury was a great coping skill, but she also didn't make me feel bad about it or try to spend too much time correcting the behavior.

Dr. Jill wanted to know about my life, my feelings, and what had happened to stir my emotions in the past. She encouraged journaling as a way to get my emotions out, which I have continued to use as a release ever since.

I had six sessions that summer before I left for university. These sessions freed me up to talk about whatever was on my mind; I did not fear any of it getting back to my parents or being used against me.

When I began to cry in a session, I would work hard to stop. One day, Dr. Jill looked at me with her kind eyes and said, "Why are you working so hard at not crying?"

"I don't want to be weak," I said, still fighting tears.

"Stephanie, there is no weakness in tears. It's the body's way of cleansing and getting emotions out. Crying is very important to life and recovery. I would like you to work on letting yourself cry at least once a week. There is emotional freedom in it." I did work on crying and sharing my feelings. But there was only so much progress I could make in the six sessions we had, as I had twenty years of emotions to work through.

At the end of the summer, I was as ready as I could be to venture into my new life in Orlando, my Volvo tightly packed with my belongings. But before I left, my friends threw me a surprise going-away party. I had never had a true surprise party before, and they really made me feel special. As most of them were staying in Tallahassee for college, it was a big deal that I was leaving the group. We had been so close for so long, and no one knew what the future held for our friendships.

When the time came, my parents drove down with me and helped me move into UCF. My dorm was brand new and apartment-style, with my own room and bathroom and a shared kitchen and living room. Three other roommates shared the common space. It was the best of dorm life on campus, so I was thrilled it was available. My parents left and, for the first time, I was truly on my own.

CHAPTER FIVE

37 Hours

A t 7 p.m., sitting quietly by myself in the CRC waiting room, I finally got word that I was being transferred to the Psychiatric Intensive Treatment Unit at the Florida Hospital Center for Behavioral Health.

As my transfer vehicle pulled up to this new location, I noticed that the surrounding area was pretty, with a lake and picnic table. I thought, *Maybe this is a treatment center like in the Sandra Bullock movie* 28 Days.

That's one of my favorite movies, and I love Sandra's performance. The movie is about people with different issues: alcohol, drugs, relationships, and self-harm. They all end up in a treatment center and grow close through group meetings and working and living together. When they finish treatment, they keep in contact because of the deep connections they made. The movie made it look like an intense summer camp.

Well, if this place is anything like that movie, maybe it won't be so bad, I thought.

I walked in, and I felt calm. The hallway was very medical but also had a homey touch. My handlers dropped me off and left. Three smiling faces took my things and escorted me inside the treatment unit. *Okay, not too bad*, I thought. It was a hospital, but it was certainly better than the run-down CRC.

My first step: another medical examination. A female nurse unwrapped my arm, took a look, and wrapped it back. Then she took some tubes of blood and got my temperature. She made me pull off my scrubs to see if I had cut my legs as well. It felt humiliating to take my scrubs off in front of her, mainly because she didn't believe me when I told her it was only my arm. When she could see I was telling the truth, she proceeded to lead me to the dining room.

On our way there, I looked around and noticed the hospital was very sterile and cold. Literally cold—I felt like I was outside on a winter day. We arrived at the dining room, which was a big open space with round tables and a few chairs around them. About twelve people sat at the tables, all in different spots. More than half of them were just staring at the TV.

I found an empty table and ate dinner around 7:30 p.m. About this time, Matt found me and we talked one on one in person! Matt didn't know anything about what was happening to me, but he knew me and he cared. He told me he was at CRC when I got the dove note. He was right outside the whole time. They wouldn't let him see me, but he finally convinced them to give me his note. It warmed my heart knowing he was there with me. As we chatted, I was so curious about how he had found me. He shared the story.

My mom had called Matt, as she knew he was in the Orlando area. My mom made this happen. My mom couldn't be with me herself, so she had found a way to help comfort me from afar.

After a short while, a nurse gave me my clothes in a brown bag. "Do I get to put them on?" I asked. My excitement was audible. A shred of humanity was being given back to me!

Then I remembered all I had in the bag was shorts and a T-shirt, and that was not going to cut it in the cold box I now lived in. I expressed this to Matt as he left. He said he would be back soon with some warmer clothes for me.

A male nurse asked if I needed anything special. A toothbrush, toothpaste, and oh yeah, pads, I told him; my period had started while I was at CRC. He escorted me to the supply room and gave me a bucket for my toiletries. He also gave me slipper socks because all I had arrived in were flip-flops.

Next, he showed me to my room. It was a decent size—two twin beds on the back wall with a window in the middle. The window had thick bars in front of it, and the glass was hard to see through. I could sort of see the outside from it. There was a wide-open space in the middle of the room and a bathroom on the right side.

The male nurse left me in the room so I could change. I looked inside the bathroom. *Oh gosh*, I thought, *a metal toilet. Now, I can definitely say a mental hospital and prison are not so different.*

When I had left my dorm room a little more than twenty-four hours ago, not knowing where I was going or for how long, I just had on a short-sleeve T-shirt and shorts. I had changed out of my scrubs and back into those clothes. It was nice to be me again, but I was hardcore freezing now!

When I emerged from the bathroom, a girl was sitting on one of the beds. *My roommate*, I assumed. I sat on the other bed and introduced myself. She talked; I tried to be friendly. Her name was Nicole. She was thirty, bipolar, schizophrenic, and had attention deficit hyperactivity disorder. She told me about her son. He was taken from her, and she was going through a divorce.

As Nicole talked, a loud alarm sounded. I thought it was a fire alarm, so I got up to go, but Nicole told me to stay seated. "The sound means someone is probably trying to hurt themselves, and it alerts the staff," she said.

Suddenly, I saw a ton of people rush to a room right outside our door. A loud beep went off when a team of about ten male nurses entered the room. I heard a man yelling and what sounded like him shaking on a bed, as if he was in pain and trying to get free. I heard the nurses rush to him and hold him down.

Then the alarm stopped. I assumed they had sedated the man with a drug. I never saw him. I don't know what was wrong with him, but this process happened many times during my stay at the hospital.

After this, Nicole went right back to talking about her life. She acted as if alarms were pretty normal around here, which was not comforting.

As we talked, a male patient walked into our room. He was skinny and disheveled and had droopy, devilish eyes. He asked if we wanted to have sex. I froze.

Why was this crazy man allowed to just walk into our room? There were no workers around, and I didn't know what this man might do.

My whole life, I've had a fear of being raped. I don't know where it came from. I've always been pretty strong and can hold my own, but this fear of being overpowered and taken advantage of by a man had always been there in the back of my head.

As I quietly panicked, Nicole started yelling at him, "Get out! Get out! I will push the alarm on you!"

She started walking toward the wall that had a big red button, which I was noticing for the first time.

That's good to know, I thought. *I wish the nurses had mentioned the emergency button before.*

The man finally left, although I will never forget his crazy, dirty eyes staring at me. Nicole acted like it was pretty normal and said it was snack time in the dining room.

She left the room, and I was a little afraid and a little excited to be alone. I organized my things and after thirty seconds, I had nothing left to do. So, I just lay on my bed, which felt like a bad camping cot.

Later, I went to the front desk and asked to call my dad. The "desk" was a fully enclosed box in the middle of the hospital unit. It had a few windows, which had to be opened if the nurses wanted to communicate with patients. I knocked on a window and waited for one to reply. I asked if I could make a phone call.

"Local or long distance?" the nurse said with a sigh.

"Long distance, I guess. My parents are in Tallahassee."

"We have to patch it through to the phones on the wall. Write down the number and wait by the phone for it to ring." She sounded bothered by my request.

Three phones hung on the wall outside the nurses' box. They looked like old-style pay phones, only there was nowhere to put money and they were not encased in a booth. I waited about fifteen minutes until one finally rang.

"Hello?" I said.

"Hello," my dad said on the other end.

"Hi, Dad. I'm at a mental hospital now, and the people here are really crazy. Like alarms going off and talking to people in their head crazy! I shouldn't be here. I'm not going to get the help I need here. I need to get out. You need to do something! Call them and tell them I shouldn't be here!" I pleaded in a progressively more panicked voice.

"Stephanie, you need to calm down. There's nothing I can do. You need to play the game, and you will get out. I know how this works and if you are frantic and crying, they will not release you. You need to be calm and do what they say. They will not keep you long; there is no reason. They have plenty of patients they need to see, and you will not be kept long," Dr. Lawrence said.

I just wanted him to be my dad. I had enough "medical professionals" around me, and I didn't need him giving me the same company line.

I thought, *It's easy for him to say, "Stay calm" while he talks to me on the phone from the comfort of his house.*

"Play the game"—a sports metaphor. I always sucked at sports. I was on the junior varsity basketball team in high school for a year. Try as we did, we never won a game. That was our legacy: We never even won *one* game. So, why would this game be any different? What would winning even look like in this game?

After feeling defeated by Dr. Lawrence, I just wanted to go to bed. I entered my room to find clothes on my bed with a note from Matt. The sight of the care package made me smile.

Matt's note said that he was not good at shopping for women's clothes, but he had tried. He had bought me a sweatshirt, shirt, leggings, underwear, and night clothes. He also got me a book, Sudoku, and a notebook. It warmed my freezing body to see the care Matt went through to bring me these things.

I didn't have a pen to write in the notebook, so I walked to the office to ask for one. After many requests, I was offered a golf pencil.

As I was waiting for the pencil, I saw Nicole yelling on the phone and saying she wanted a "twenty-four-hour release form." I understood it was something about her child and divorce case. She was going to lose custody of her kid. She wanted to leave to get the problem worked out.

I went to my room to start writing this story, and then I went to sleep. Although the camping cot was not comfortable, I was so tired so I slept well.

● ● ● ● ●

At 6 a.m. Tuesday morning, I was rudely awakened to have my blood taken. After that, I wasn't told what to do, so I just hung out in my room waiting for further instructions. I sat on my bed and continued to write this story.

At 9 a.m., a grad student arrived and took me to a small room. She told me to tell her what had happened and that she would report it back to the psychiatrist. It frustrated me that I didn't get to talk to the psychiatrist myself, but I didn't let that show. I tried to be human, calm, and funny. I retold my story. She finished up and told me it was time for group session and that I was free to go.

Not having any clue what group session was or where it was, I walked to my room and waited to see the psychiatrist myself, hoping he would allow me to go home. The psychiatrist was the head honcho here, so I thought he might be the person with the power to release me. I was hopeful that after talking with him, he would agree I didn't need to be in this facility.

I was called in to see him five hours later ... and my meeting lasted all of five minutes. First, he looked me up and down and said, "What are you wearing?"

His question shocked me. *Why do you care?* I thought to myself.

He was not the first to ask me this. I didn't feel comfortable wearing just the leggings Matt had bought me, so I had put my shorts over them.

My "look" was a white sweatshirt, black leggings with green Bermuda shorts, and slipper socks. Based on everyone's reaction, it was not a positive fashion statement. But you know, it kept me warm, and that's all that mattered to me!

As I was sharing my story, the psychiatrist started looking at his papers and began writing. He didn't seem to care about listening to me. He stopped my talking by putting his hand in the air, palm toward me, and said he wanted me on Seroquel and Zoloft. Then he said he wanted to observe how I would do on the drugs.

He wants me to take drugs and observe. That takes time, I thought.

He didn't even hear my full story. He didn't even know my history. It was as if he didn't see me as an individual; it was as if he saw me as another body and his job was to drug it and see what happens.

After my brain quickly processed this information, I told him I didn't want to take the drugs. I just needed to get out to deal with my problems through therapy.

He said, "You have to take the drugs if you want to be released. They are part of the treatment plan. The medication will be ready for you to take right after dinner."

I knew what Zoloft was but had never heard of Seroquel, so I asked him if he could explain to me what it was for and what it would do to/for me. He gave me a piece of paper that explained what Seroquel was and sent me on my way.

I read the sheet in my room: Seroquel is used for the treatment of schizophrenia; it is also indicated for the short-term treatment of acute manic episodes associated with bipolar I disorder in adults.

After reading the whole sheet, I did feel crazy. This doc must think I'm schizophrenic or bipolar if he wants me on this drug! The doc never told me any of this. He just said he wanted me on the drug. What's a girl to think after reading what the drug is for?

At that moment, I began to think that I might really be "crazy." Maybe I do hear voices. Maybe I'm bipolar. Maybe this was a manic episode. I know I have depression, but maybe there is more.

I started to panic; I wanted the crazy out! I called my dad to tell him what was going on and that they wanted to "drug" me. Again, he said to play the game and I would get out faster.

"This is my body, and they want me to drug it!" I yelled.

"It's a low dose. It won't affect you," he said.

"Then why take it at all?" I yelled again.

"It's part of the process. You don't have to keep taking them once you're out," Dad said, sounding annoyed.

I was so mad at his words. I yelled at him some more, slammed the phone down, and went to my room crying. I was furious! A nurse came in to see me because of the scene I had just made.

"I'm fine!" I yelled. Nurse Johnny tried to calm me. I yelled my side of the story through tears and anger.

"No one is helping me! I want my bandage changed and I have been waiting since last night and it's still not done! I have a simple request. I wait patiently, and I get treated like I'm invisible!" I told Johnny.

"We have other patients who are a higher priority," he said.

"I know. That's why I shouldn't be here—because you don't have time for me," I said sadly.

"I'm sorry you feel that way, but that's how it is," Johnny said.

We went on to have an intelligent debate about the treatment of patients in the hospital. I tried to find my sane place to present my arguments with facts and clarity. In the end, Johnny bounced it all back on me, saying that if I wanted to get out, having a "fit" was not the way to do it.

It's all a f*** game, I thought to myself.

All I kept thinking was that I didn't cut myself to play. I cut out of frustration. Not suicide, not for attention, not for punishing others—but to have control of my out-of-control life. I felt so much confusion, pain, and anger. Self-injury was a way to pinpoint the pain—"Here is where it hurts."

As Johnny and I sat on my bed in silence for a moment, I looked over at Nicole's bed. I told Johnny I felt bad for her because she was losing custody of her kid and was not able to get out to fight for him.

He looked at me, silent for a moment, then laughed a little and said, "You know, she doesn't have a kid. She's not married and never has been. All that is made up—part of her illness."

I sat shocked. I had believed everything she told me. I felt mad and confused.

Is she someone who really needs to be in the mental hospital, and is she getting the right help? I wondered.

Johnny left the room and returned with gauze to redo my bandage. He told me he had undergone surgical training, so he knew how to clean my arm and wrap it. I felt very safe in his hands. He also told me that peroxide loosens stitches, which made me mad because that's what they poured all over my arm at CRC, right after the stitches were put in.

After the talk, I felt better. I was happy to be told what was going on and to feel as if I was adult enough to understand my own life.

But I was still concerned about the drugs and if I should take them, so I called Dr. Jill. She told me, "They drug everyone because they want the patients zoned out and zombielike. It's easier to control the situation that way."

"Considering what the drugs are for, I must be schizophrenic or bipolar," I told Dr. Jill.

She was quiet a moment.

"Stephanie, you do not have those mental illnesses. They don't have the time or the resources in that place to really help you."

This was comforting to hear, but it didn't change the fact that I was still locked up.

CHAPTER SIX

74 Hours

waited patiently outside the nurses' box for visiting hours to begin. My roommate Megan had called me earlier in the day to tell me she would be coming to see me. She would be bringing two things I really needed: a quality toothbrush and two-ply toilet paper. Megan and I had just met a few months before but had become fast friends. We shared a lot about our personal lives; I had told her about my history with self-injury. Megan was so different from me, but we respected each other and our differences.

When Megan arrived, I jumped up and down inside my head with glee. We made light of the hospital, laughed, and played human for an hour. I told her about Nicole and some of the people I had met. She asked me what she should tell people if they asked where I was.

I said, "I don't care. Whatever you want."

"How about I tell them you're at Nicole's Place?" Megan said.

"Ha, that's a good code word for it," I said. "I like it. Nicole's Place it is!"

After Megan left, I headed to dinner. In the dining room, a new guy told me that I looked like his daughter. He was probably in his forties or fifties and looked like he had done a lot of living. His face was worn from the things he had seen. I couldn't see it at first because we were sitting down, but he showed me where he had a chunk shot out of his leg in a war. His whole calf was missing. It looked strange. How could he still walk? He seemed pretty normal; he had just lived a lot of life. I never asked what he was in the hospital for.

Right after dinner, all the patients lined up outside the nurses' drive-through style window. Slowly, one by one, patients picked up a cup full of pills, swallowed them, then showed the nurse they had done so. This moment seemed the craziest of all to me. If this was all a game—a very dangerous one since it involved human life—I decided to play and take the drugs.

As I got closer to the window, I felt like I was losing myself. *Will I be completely zoned out after taking these drugs? Will I forget what's going on? Will I keep trying so hard? Will I not want to try anymore?*

And there I was. It was my turn. A nurse handed me a cup with two pills inside it. I swallowed, and that was it.

As I lay in my bed with the drugs slowly entering my bloodstream, I couldn't get to sleep. I thought about how strange it was that no one wanted to examine why I coped with self-injury. No one asked about my past and the feelings that brought it on.

They focused so much on "my roommate ate my food, so I cut my arm." What a dumbed-down version of the story. No one was curious enough to dig deeper and help me discover why I was scarred.

I spent a lot of time trying to figure out how to explain the feelings I have when my brain tells me to cope with self-injury. It's so hard to explain with simple words. It's something I just feel. I don't intellectualize it. But I tried to think of an example.

First, imagine that a typical person has an event come into their head. Maybe they learned they got into college or had a fight with a friend. These events would register in their brain, and the brain would send these events to the heart to interpret the proper emotion to feel. The heart would tell the brain what to feel, and with the brain and heart aligned, that person would go through the proper emotion for each event.

In my case, imagine one of those same events occurred. My brain knows I need to feel something, so it sends it down to my heart. But my heart is not there. My organs are not there. My body is an empty shell, so the event just bounces around, desperate to get resolved. After a while, my brain realizes it hasn't heard from my heart about what emotion to feel.

Then my brain starts to go into overdrive, trying to figure out on its own what to do about the event. But my brain doesn't know how to determine the emotion on its own. What my brain *does* know is this: "When I see a cut on the body, I instantly feel pain in that area."

So, my brain, knowing it needs to tell me how to feel about the event, tells me to cut my arm to feel emotion. So, I cut, and I feel pain in that one area. My lost brain, without its heart, is semi-satisfied. This goes on like a ritual. For good and bad events, this is the process every time my brain needs me to feel. After my brain shut down my heart years ago, it never went back.

But where did my heart go? Why is my body out of sync? Why has this misalignment happened?

As I drifted off to sleep, this next part was more dreamlike. Something big and unimaginable must have happened to me long ago that was too big for my heart. My brain took it in and sent it to my heart. My heart told it how to feel, but it was too much for my brain. It was too much for my brain to handle, and it told my heart *no*. It told my heart it would not feel that, and it shut her down.

But even with my heart shut down, that childhood event still happened. That event is still inside, unresolved, deep inside my brain. It lives in my subconscious, and it very much has an impact on everything I do.

So, how do I sync them back up? I have to learn what made my brain cut out my heart. What event caused this failed sync to happen? My brain is not so easily tapped into. It's going to protect me as best it can. It's going to continue to distract me. It's going to continue to give me false readings of my emotions and how to handle them.

But there is something bigger than my simple brain. God is always superior to me. He is the One who can open up my brain and show me what I need to know and, ultimately, realign my brain and heart.

But at twenty years old, I was not ready to learn about what really happened in my childhood. I was unaware of the magnitude behind my self-injury coping method. At the time, I thought self-injury was the issue I needed to resolve. Little did I know that when I stopped focusing on self-injury, then the real healing would begin. But that would not come till years later.

• • • • •

The next thing I knew, a nurse woke me up on Wednesday morning by poking and prodding for my blood and temperature. So far, the drugs didn't seem to have a noticeable effect.

Around 10 a.m. I was assigned a social worker. She was the first person who treated me kindly; care and compassion flowed from her eyes. She didn't pass judgment, even after I shared how I had ended up in the hospital. She said it would add positively to my case if I attended group session. She said I would also get to go outside in the session—which I really needed. I had been cooped up like a caged animal way too long.

I headed to group session in the craft room. Once there, I saw stuff everywhere. It looked like elementary students had been in the room; supplies, paintings, and drawings were sprawled around. It smelled of paint and chemicals. About twenty patients and two workers occupied the room.

One patient was a very tall man I recognized from the day before. When he came to the hospital, he was talking to voices around him. It was pretty scary. He wasn't in control then. But today, he looked better.

He must have been given drugs to mellow him out, I thought.

We all sat around a table with a worksheet titled "It's Never Too Early … or Late … to Take 21 Steps to … Aging Successfully!"

I started this painfully elementary exercise. One of the questions: "How often do you touch nature?" Our instructors asked us what it meant to "touch nature." I had already answered a few questions, so I didn't offer my suggestion.

About an hour later, everyone was finished with the worksheet and I was about to pull my teeth out from boredom. I received a score of 98 percent, which was even higher than the instructor's score.

Fabulous. Can we go outside to "touch nature" now? I thought.

We did go outside next, but I'm not sure you can even call it outside. We were escorted to a small patio area surrounded on top and all sides with a chain link fence. I could barely see the outside; I certainly could not "touch nature."

The patio contained a basketball hoop, a volleyball net, and a few game balls in bags. I played a game of scoop ball with one of the patients. If nothing else, at least the air was fresh.

After group session, I was really over it. I sat on the plastic bench in front of the nurses' office to wait for any word on my release.

I had taken the drugs and told my story. I had played nice with the group; now was the time to get my life back! I waited for hours. I was told it would be today. But at that point, I had learned not to trust. Megan had said she would come pick me up as soon as she got the call.

As I waited, I read a Bible that the psychiatric-unit pastor had given me. After a while, I looked up, and the dark, tall man I recognized from today's group session appeared next to me. When I saw him yesterday, I had been scared because he had clearly been talking to people who were not there. In group, he had talked about voices telling him to do bad things like commit crimes and take drugs. As he approached me today, I tensed up. But I could see a change in him. I saw him and only him. He saw me reading, and his face lit up.

"Where did you get that Bible?" he asked kindly.

"The pastor here gave it to me. I bet he will give you one too. Just ask," I explained.

He seemed excited and went to see how he could talk to the pastor. As I continued to sit, I thought over the moment I had with that man and kicked myself for not giving him my Bible.

Lost in my thoughts, I almost didn't understand when they gave me the good news: I was to be released! I expressed my gratitude calmly and waited for Megan.

As I continued to wait, I saw the man walking and realized it was now or never. I walked over to him and handed him the Bible. I told him it was his now. He stared straight into my eyes, with tears in his. He took my hands and said, "God bless you." I smiled, and we stood silent for a moment. Then I returned to my bench with tears in my eyes. That was a real human moment I will never forget.

Around 5 p.m. Wednesday, I was released. I signed the forms and received my phone and wallet back. My roommate Megan showed up, and I was free in the world again. It was strange to think how quickly my freedom had been taken away.

I just wanted the past four days washed away from my memory, as if they never happened. I wanted to move forward again. Megan took me to Wendy's, where I got a sandwich, Frosty with treats, and a salad. We headed back to our dorm. That was it. It was all over ... or so I thought.

PART 2

Abuse

CHAPTER SEVEN

Aftermath

was held in the system for seventy-four hours. That's fifty hours more than if I had been Baker Acted (involuntarily) admitted. I trusted the people I thought were there to protect and help me. My parents raised me to look at police officers and medical professionals with respect. This experience taught me a hard life lesson. Life isn't as simple as "trust the safe people."

The experience hardened me and made me fearful of new people, especially people meant to "help" me. I was fearful that they would judge me unfairly and make me feel like the crazy one. Because of this, I didn't see another doctor for five years, except for when I got my stitches removed after my stay at

Nicole's Place. I had googled a doctor who was covered by my insurance near UCF. I hadn't bothered to get a local doctor yet, as I had only lived in Orlando a few months. I found one right down the road and made an appointment to get my stitches removed.

I walked into the tiny white room, with the standard cotton balls and tongue depressors on the counter, and sat on the medical table. I waited. An older male doctor walked into the room, looked a little perturbed, and asked to see the stitches.

I showed him my arm. His eyes widened a little, then he looked into my face. I looked back and saw disdain, frustration, and apathy. He unhappily went to get his tools, then came back and, without a word, started removing the stitches. I was sitting up, with my arm in my lap.

His pulling and prodding my arm felt unusual. It upset me. The sensation made me lightheaded. I told him I didn't feel good. He continued and said, "Well, what do you expect? It's a lot of stitches!"

He must have finally looked at my face and saw it turning pale, so he told me to lie down on the table. This helped, and he finished his task. He never asked me what happened. I can only imagine he looked at my arm as a failed suicide attempt. His pessimistic attitude made me feel like I was wasting the time he could be using to see "real" patients.

• • • • •

In the days and weeks following my release from Nicole's Place, I tried to get back to normal. I returned to my classes (although I missed a test in film class and my teacher wouldn't let me make it up). I went back to my weekly Bible study and shared a surface-level version of what happened. And I attended sorority events again.

I felt shame for what I had done and put my family, friends, and roommates through. I never *really* talked about the nightmare Nicole's Place was or showed anyone the writing I did there.

A few days after my release, the bill for my stay arrived in the mail. It led with "Thank you for choosing Florida Hospital for your health care needs."

Thank you? I thought. *Really? Like I had a choice!*

The grand total came to $11,970.78 for the four days. Of course, this was the price they billed my insurance, but the bill made me furious. To see how much money they charged, and the lack of any helpful treatment, showed me that it's a broken system. In the end, my parents' co-pay was about $600. To this day, I'm upset they paid it.

Along the same lines, UCF sent a note to my parents stating, "Stephanie was transported to the hospital after engaging in harmful behavior. Students need to assume responsibility for their actions; however, parents play a very important role in addressing consequences of their student's behavior."

It was just an extra punch in the gut. After reading it, I thought, *I guess UCF didn't get the memo that my parents were talking with me through the whole ordeal and that my mom spent time with me afterwards. But, you know, if the kid already feels bad about herself, make sure the parents do too!*

I also received a letter from UCF eight days after I got back. The letter stated that my university records would be put on hold if I did not go and speak with the Director of Student Conduct. Even without the threat, I would have complied. I did go. I did everything I was asked and told to do. I went to UCF mandatory counseling. But all the "help" I got was checking boxes off a list for the school.

The final embarrassment and shame for me was having to go to required roommate mediation. I don't remember much about it, but I remember AJ's face. She hated every minute of it and hated me. I think this goes without saying, but this did not help my relationship with AJ or DeeDee.

The checklist UCF had me go through did nothing to help me work on my feelings, fear, and shock from those seventy-four hours. The more people treated me like a mental patient, the more I started to feel like one. And I hated myself for what

A view down from my sitting tree in the woods

I did … to myself, as I was always reminded. I needed real help, but I was too scared to ask for it. I was so afraid I would be sent back to Nicole's Place.

One day, I took a walk in the woods right outside my dorm room. It had beautiful paths of undeveloped land with amazing trees and natural life. Instantly, I fell in love and didn't feel so afraid and alone anymore. I felt close to God, surrounded by His creations. With His help, I processed some of my feelings through frequent trips to the woods.

• • • • •

Police Officer Moen Facebook-friended me when I left Nicole's Place. He wanted to check up on me and see how I was. I was friendly, but in the back of my mind I always wondered, *Did you really think I was a danger to myself or others? Did you think I was suicidal? Did you know anything about CRC, and did you honestly think I would get the right treatment?* After seven years of being too afraid to ask the questions, I finally did. I know I'm getting a little ahead of the story, but this is what he said:

> "To answer your questions honestly, at the time, I did what I was required to do in the situation that was presented. I had a very basic explanation of what CRC was from a class I had attended. As far as treatment, I cannot speak to that as I never got that far in the process. I was directed that if a person did or said certain things, this was the process we followed. I know this is not a good answer and doesn't even begin to explain the why of what occurred.
>
> I can imagine it was an ordeal for you and caused a major disruption in your life and I am sorry if it was the wrong decision in your case, but my hands were tied regarding how I was to handle the situation. I have remained in contact with you mainly because I wanted to be there for you as a resource if you needed anything."

This was helpful closure for me.

• • • • •

When I began attending UCF, I decided to go through sorority rush week. I never, and I mean *never*, wanted to be a "sorority girl" growing up. My mom was one when she was in college and loved it. She said it was like Girl Scouts but better. She didn't ask or encourage me to join, but I knew it would make her happy if I became a member of her sorority. So, I went through the process and got accepted. All that happened before the seventy-four hours. I didn't tell anyone in the sorority about Nicole's Place.

One month after my release from that facility, it was time to be initiated into the sorority. My mom came down for the November ceremony. I didn't know what to expect. Mom said it was no big deal and that I would be fine. Well, it would prove to be the stereotype of a sorority initiation.

In the two-story sorority house, they blindfolded us and made us find our way to the rooms on the second floor. Then they left us three to a room with the lights out. There I was, sitting on the floor facing a shut window with a desk in front of it. They left us for hours—nothing to do—and strange noises were coming from the hallway. We were told to sit on the floor, stay, and shut up.

As I sat for hours, I noticed a shirt on the desk chair in front of me. It was white with little black skulls printed in a pattern. Two other people sat behind me in the room, but I couldn't see them so I felt all alone.

As I stared at the little black skulls, my mind and body reacted in panic and fear, but *not* because of the stupid sorority game. It was because I felt like I was back in the place where I was held captive for four days. The tiny room I now sat in became the hospital—locked up against my will, not allowed to leave. The strange noises in the hallway became the hospital alarms and patients crying out in pain. My sorority "sisters" became the nurses.

"Shut up, and do what I say," they told me.

I was drowning in the flashback of Nicole's Place—not knowing what was happening, being told what to do, where to go, and with no power over my own life. I tried to stay calm and remind myself where I was, but it was no use. As long as I stayed in that space, the flashback would swallow me whole.

I couldn't take it anymore! I stood up with tears in my eyes. Girls told me to sit back down. I didn't listen. I left the room. This was not a game anymore, and these blonde Barbies were not going to control me. I told those outside the room to get my mom. They said she had already gone through the ritual and was in the ceremony room.

"I don't give a f*** about this ritual game," I screamed. "Get her out!" The shocked sorority girls complied, and my mom came out.

Through tears, I told her what happened, what they did, and the flashback I'd had. In time, she calmed me. She realized that this was not the sorority she remembered. The years had turned it into something else, something less pure and not true to the founders' vision.

"Steph, you don't have to go through initiation. I'm really fine if you don't," Mom told me kindly.

"I've come this far; I want to follow through," I said.

Ultimately, I did go through with the ceremony. I knew everyone would have heard what I did by that time, but I was too wiped out from the experience to be embarrassed.

In the end, I finally got to learn the secret sorority handshake and password. Though I'd never had an interest in joining a sorority, for years I had wanted to see into this mysterious world. I had wanted to know the secrets. If only I had done a quick Google search all those years ago, I would have found the full initiation instructions with secrets online!

When I was younger, my parents would make me and my brother stay at least a year at something we had committed to. One year, I wanted to quit Girl Scouts. I don't remember why. But Mom made me stay till the end of the year. Well, that year came to a close and I decided to continue with Scouts, and I was so glad I did.

This experience taught me that it was important to give the sorority at least a year. I continued to go to meetings and participate—but in my mind, I was done. I even produced the recruitment video for the next rush week. But by the end of the school year, I knew I couldn't do it anymore. I never set foot in the sorority house again.

CHAPTER EIGHT

Apple

n the summer of 2007, I walked into the Apple store in the Mall at Millenia in Orlando. I was looking for a new monitor. I had been in this Apple store once before, in 2004, when I came with my friends for our Disney spring break trip. The store was even better than I remembered. It was nice and open, with wood fixtures and all the Apple products on display. I wanted it all! But I headed to the monitors.

Jeff walked up to me wearing a black Apple T-shirt with a clever phrase and asked what I was looking for. We got to talking about how I use my Mac. I shared my passion for video editing and how much the software Final Cut Pro was part of my workflow. My pure passion blew Jeff away. With much passion of his own, he said that I needed to work for Apple. This sounded like a dream, so of course, I applied. Oh, and I got the job!

A few months before, I had been hired by Walt Disney World to work at its Indiana Jones Epic Stunt Spectacular! show. Don't get excited—I didn't do stunts, but I could pack the audience into the theater with perfection!

So, in my last year of college, I filled all my time with classes, an internship, Disney, *and* Apple. I have no idea how I did it all, but I did and enjoyed it. It felt good to have places to be, to have jobs to do, and to have purpose. When I was working, no one knew about Nicole's Place. No one knew what I had experienced and seen; they just knew I was a good worker.

As for my arm, I covered my scars with skin-colored patches, special makeup, or an armband. One of my positions at Disney was to hold my arms up at my sides and point left and right with my fingers. This fully exposed my scars to everyone walking into the theater. It gave me a lot of anxiety whenever I was assigned this position, but no one ever said anything to me about my scars.

When I graduated college in winter of 2008, I was promoted to a full-time position as a Creative at Apple. My job there was not exactly video production, but as a Creative I taught "One to One" customers how to use Final Cut Pro, among other software. It kept my production need satisfied a little. It felt so good to teach and see someone grow and learn in just one hour.

At the time Apple hired me, I was one of just a handful of women employees at my store. That didn't seem strange to me, as I was typically one of the only females in my various jobs.

Our store leader was a woman, which was nice but we never saw her in the store. Then one day, in August 2009, we found out that our store leader had left Apple to work for Microsoft. She had taken half of our employees with her. It was shocking and devastating.

I am very loyal and did not work for Apple for the money, though that was nice and important. I worked for Apple because I believed in the products, the brand, and the corporate leadership. It felt like a personal attack when those employees left. I felt like there were enemies among me the whole time, and I never knew it.

Soon after these employees left, the position of Lead Creative became available. This person's role was to lead the creative team of about seven people. I had a passion for the store and team and thought I could do some good. My fellow Creatives encouraged me to apply, so I did. I prepared so much for that interview. Once I made up my mind, I knew I was the right person for the job.

As our store leader was gone, one of the long-time managers, Shawn, became acting store leader. I'd never had a good feeling about Shawn. I always felt a little uncomfortable around him, but I didn't know why. I didn't let that affect the job interview, however, and I rocked it.

One day, Shawn called me into the manager's office and told me the good news: I got the job! I would be getting a big pay increase of 10 percent.

I didn't know what to say. Ten percent was like two dollars more an hour than I was making as a Creative. Lead Creative had completely different responsibilities.

I said, "That's it? Ten percent doesn't sound right. I'm going to bring so much value to this role as I laid out in my business plan during the interview."

Shawn looked at me very matter-of-fact and said, "Ten percent is the standard pay increase for this position. I don't have the authority to change that."

"Well, who *does* have the authority? We don't have a store leader, so who is in charge?" I asked.

"I could talk to the store leader at the Florida Mall Apple store if you want," Shawn said dryly.

"Yes, please. Can I talk to her?"

"No. I'll handle it and let you know," Shawn said.

After all that, two things saddened me: One, this was the first time I really felt discriminated against for being a woman. Two, Shawn came back to me with a puny 15 percent raise—final offer.

Since I was already being paid on the low scale for a Creative, the raise was still not significant. But I took it because I felt defeated, ashamed, and wanted to be done with the fight.

As Lead Creative, I was the youngest on the leadership team. My responsibilities quickly grew when I went from overseeing just Creatives to the whole family room, which was made of about fifty people. Many days, my responsibilities and the metrics we needed to hit overwhelmed me.

I still struggled with self-injury. I still struggled with depression. I still, deep down, was scared I would be sent back to Nicole's Place. But I pushed through all those feelings and spent my days laser-focused on my job. I didn't focus on a personal life. I focused on being the best Lead Creative I could be.

That started with me developing my own leadership skills. I spent many hours reading about leadership, business, and how to develop a team. I planned an outdoor team-building activity, where we spent half a day in a park learning to trust and encourage each other. The team went to the opening of LEGOLAND, and for the holidays we visited Mickey's Very Merry Christmas Party at Magic Kingdom.

I did my very best and tried to earn the respect of my team. But as hard as I tried, some team members still saw me as "the man." One day on the sales floor, I was standing off to the side with my iPad checking the schedule to see who needed to take their break. I was in earshot of a group from the Family Room Team. They were talking about this and that, and then I heard my name. And I heard them all agree that I was a "b" word. Previously, my coworker and friend Jason told me he had overheard them call me this, but it hit much harder hearing it for myself.

It's just a word, but it was used in a mean and hateful way. It punched me right in the gut, and I had a rush of emotions that I didn't know what to do with. But I was at work, on the sales floor, so I pushed down my emotions and went to help customers. I distracted myself with work during the whole shift. When I got home, I lost it.

I was fully crying and couldn't stop. Jason came over, and I just lay in the backseat of his car as he drove around and I vented. I felt defeated. He drove me to Sonic and got me a limeade, which is my fav.

On the drive home, I was still lamenting what my team had said about me. Then it hit me: Do kids always like their parents? Do kids say mean things to them? Most people don't like authority and the person they have to report to.

"Maybe I am a 'b' and maybe that's okay. Maybe a 'b' is someone who stands up for herself, doesn't back down, and does the job that needs to be done, in the way it needs to be done," I told Jason.

I dried my tears. Just a few people had uttered those words about me, not the whole team. Some team members *did* respect me, and I had bosses who were proud of me. I was not going to let this group of people bring me down. This was the first time I really had to address haters in my life. This experience has served me well, especially with social media and online haters.

I did have a group of cheerleaders on my team—Jason being one, and Daniel being another. When Daniel was hired, every interaction I had with him truly impressed me. He was so positive. Even if the store was on fire and we were stuck and couldn't get out, he would have stayed positive—and figured out a way to get us out!

Along with his genuinely amazing attitude, he was also encouraging. He had no time for haters and always put into perspective what a great job I was doing. He was, and is, my loudest cheerleader!

Even more inspiring for me is the fact that he has Type 1 diabetes and never lets it slow him down. I've always been in awe of how much this affects his life, but his attitude is still the same. He has to constantly be on top of his health, or he could pass out or worse. Still, he lives to the fullest and welcomes each day with open arms and excitement.

Daniel's friendship and kind spirit helped me look inward and see my own struggles. I began to see my anxiety, depression, and self-injury less as burdens and more just as parts of me. I started to wonder, *How can I live my best life and not let my mental issues define me?*

Me at work, photo by Daniel Kuykendall

• • • • •

A few years later, I had another encounter with Shawn. After serving as acting store leader, he became the business manager of the store. His job was to get business customers to switch to Macs. He's a very strong-willed salesman, so I guess it was a good role for him.

If you're not familiar with the Apple store, early on the color of team members' shirts varied depending on their job.

As Lead Creative, I wore the same shirt as my team. One day, Shawn had a great idea. He thought to bring more awareness to the business team, he would get store leaders to wear business shirts. The business team's shirts were pretty different from all the other store shirts. They were collared, made from a nice material, and were all black with a little white apple on the left sleeve.

I put on my new business shirt and went to work on December 1, 2010. Every morning, before the store opened, we had a store meeting in the back of the house. This particular morning, Shawn led the morning meeting. I happened to be standing next to him because my desk was near his. He talked about the day and, of course, reminded everyone to talk about business. He also reminded the team about the new initiative for leaders to wear business shirts. Then he turned to me, looked right in my face, put his hand on my shoulder, and announced to the whole team, "Stephanie looks so sexy in her new business shirt."

Several uncomfortable moments passed. No one knew what to say. I think even Shawn realized that what he had said was inappropriate; I just don't think he was sure why. Then he took his hand off my shoulder, nudged me in the side, and said, "I mean, you always look good … but especially good in a business shirt."

Then he looked back at the store employees as they all stared at the two of us. He closed the meeting, and the employees filtered out to the sales floor. In that moment, I went numb. I had never been sexualized in such a public way.

Everyone was gone from the back of house. I just stood there feeling ashamed, embarrassed, and used. A few of my friends came up to me afterwards and said Shawn's words made them feel uncomfortable and asked how I was. One of my good friends on the business team told me he was going to tell Shawn how inappropriate his statement was.

A few days later, Shawn did come up to me and say, "I'm sorry if I made you uncomfortable the other day. I didn't mean any harm by it."

Another employee told me that if I was that upset about it, I should report it to human resources (HR). I had no experience with sexual harassment in the workplace and what would happen, but I did contact HR. My HR rep was a man who asked me a lot of questions. I answered them as best as I could.

A month later, nothing happened. I don't know what I expected. I don't know what I wanted to happen. I had been sexually harassed in the workplace, I reported it, and that was it. I followed the process. I think HR told Shawn to apologize again. And he did, this time using lots of legal words. That's all I remember. Shawn's desk continued to be right next to mine.

I didn't realize it at the time because this happened before I learned about some sexual abuse I had endured as a child, but this moment was a flashback for me. It was a flashback that I did not understand. It was filled with feelings from my past and thoughts my brain had shut down. I can't say whether this event affected me more than it should have. I don't know if another woman in the same situation would have felt the same as me. But I know this much: What Shawn did was wrong. A few years after me, he left Apple and went to work for Microsoft.

CHAPTER NINE

43,829 Hours

I was twenty-five years old and had been physically free from Nicole's Place for 43,829 hours—in other words, five years. My body was in the free world, but my brain was not. Every day was hard. I lived in fear of going back to Nicole's Place and of what happened to me while I was there. I would hear the screams  and alarms in my head. I would feel cold and instantly be transported back to my hospital room. I wasn't free.

One thing that helped my racing brain: music. I played the song "Set Me Free" by Casting Crowns over and over during this time. I even made a video depicting scenes from my childhood, of me in my dorm room right after my release, including my fresh scars. Little did I know at the time how powerful that juxtaposition was.

Each day I felt like the shell of the person I was during the seventy-four hours of my experience five years earlier. I couldn't keep up my "I'm a happy human" show anymore. I knew something had to happen. I had to get away from work and look inward. I loved my job at Apple, but I considered quitting it because I was not sure I could get the time off that I needed.

One day, I got the courage to talk to our new store leader, Marco. He and I had a good working relationship. He respected me, my team, and my leadership. When the meeting began, I had no idea what I was going to say. All I had was mustard seed faith.

I told Marco I loved my job and wanted to keep it, but I needed some time to focus on me and my mental health. I told him I would like to take a month off and go back to Tallahassee to have some time with my doctor.

When I finished sharing, which I did calmly and concisely, he looked at my face with kindness and compassion in his. He told me I could go. I *should* go. He didn't want to lose me as an employee. He fully supported me taking time for myself. He said he would let me put my vacation and sick time together so I could go, still get paid, with my job waiting for me when I got back. This was a mustard seed moment. It was a moment that didn't seem real, but it was real because it had been God's plan for me all along.

When the time came, I packed and drove to Tallahassee in my green Honda CR-V. During the drive, I began "processing." It felt like life stopped. I was taking a break from the "path of success" we are told to travel from birth: Get a job, work, get a mate, get a house, get a kid. I pushed on the brakes. No one ever added "work on yourself." Learn to be. Take time to look inward and make sure you are mentally well, happy, and the person God made you to be.

A few days into my time away, I got ready for my session with Dr. Jill. As I took a shower that morning, I thought about how strange it seemed that I was going through all this effort to take time for myself and yet, I didn't even know what was wrong with me. But I guess that was the point, to try to figure it out with Dr. Jill. I wanted to tell her how I felt depressed all the time, how I didn't trust people, and how I had flashbacks to the hospital at random moments.

Then it hit me: Everything was related to the seventy-four hours. Everything I had been feeling these last five years could be traced back to those moments. It's as if I never left Nicole's Place and "the system" still had control over me. The memories, feelings, and overwhelming emotions had a hold on me—and brought me back to Nicole's Place every day.

As I stood in the shower with warm water pouring over my head, I had another flashback.

I was back in the ice-cold shower I had to take at Nicole's Place the first night, with my arm wrapped in plastic to protect the stitches. There were no hot and cold handles in the shower.

As I walked toward the showerhead, ice-cold water suddenly blasted down on me. It was motion activated. The water didn't begin to get warm until I was done with my shower. The feeling of complete sadness, fear, and longing to be back home filled me.

Then, just a few hours before I was to see Dr. Jill, it popped into my brain: *Is this post-traumatic stress disorder? Is that what's wrong?*

I knew PTSD was large in the military community. I knew it had to do with trauma and flashbacks and that there was a treatment plan. I pushed that thought to the back of my mind. Then I had breakfast and went to see my psychologist.

Dr. Jill had moved into her own office building since my first sessions with her. She had a small, inviting waiting room with soothing spa music playing. She called me back, and I sat on a large couch with her across from me in an armchair. I told her everything that was circling in my brain.

In the first twenty minutes, she diagnosed me with post-traumatic stress disorder. My PTSD had resulted from the seventy-four hours. When she said the words, a huge weight lifted off of me. I had a name for what I had been suffering from—and it wasn't all in my head. It was very real. It was debilitating, but we could treat it.

Now that I had my *what*—knowing what the problem was—I needed my *how*—how do I treat this? Dr. Jill told me there was not a magic pill, although I could get back on depression meds, but she didn't think they would help based on my history.

"The way you treat PTSD is to talk about the traumatic events," Dr. Jill told me.

What? I thought. *Talk? Talk about the things that tear me up inside and feel like knives jabbing through my heart if I acknowledge them?*

So simple, yet so terrifying.

Dr. Jill helped me understand that what happened to me was not right, and the hospital is at fault for my PTSD because of its lack of proper treatment. During the seventy-four hours, everyone seemed so disgusted by my wound. I just couldn't understand why this was all they focused on until I started meeting with Dr. Jill again.

She told me they thought I was trying to kill myself—a failed suicide attempt. It may seem obvious to you reading this now, but I honestly had no idea this is what everyone was thinking. For me, self-injury is unrelated to suicide. But after Dr. Jill made this connection for me, I started to see why everyone had concluded this.

Dr. Jill reminded me that I'm not a "cutter." I should have never been sent to CRC, she said, because I was not trying to kill myself or harm others. I was engaging in nonsuicidal self-injury (NSSI)—the act of feeling so much and not having physical pain to show for it. My coping was to make the internal pain real.

According to the American Psychiatric Association's DSM-5, the diagnostic feature of NSSI is an individual repeatedly inflicting shallow, yet painful injuries to the surface of his or her body. Most commonly, the purpose is to reduce negative emotions, such as tension, anxiety, and self-reproach, and/or to resolve an interpersonal difficulty. The injury is most often inflicted with a knife, needle, razor, or other sharp objects. Common areas for injury include the frontal area of the thighs and the dorsal side of the forearm. A single session of injury might involve a series of superficial, parallel cuts—separated by 1 or 2 centimeters—on a visible or accessible location.

When I read into NSSI, I realized I was a classic textbook case! It's like they wrote the diagnostic all about me. It was comforting to have an official name for my coping.

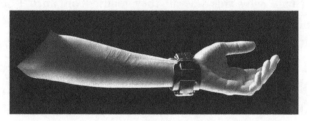

The seven scars that remain on the inside of
my left arm, photo by Daniel Kuykendall

Over the next few weeks, I followed my PTSD treatment plan. I talked. I wrote. I scribbled real and raw feelings and burned them, as Dr. Jill instructed me to do. I talked to my parents and my friends. I let it all out. Getting the hellish events out of me was freeing! So was crying. Dr. Jill liked to prescribe a good cry.

During our sessions over the month, Dr. Jill would remind me with a reassuring smile that, "You are not crazy. The police don't know how to handle these kinds of situations, so they bring all patients like this to the same place. The place you were in sounds like a place here in town, and it's not a hospital you should ever be in. They drug people and put them back on the streets."

Every session was hard. They were draining—emotionally and physically exhausting. After going through it, I knew I could have never done it while still working at Apple. Mustard seed faith helped me get to this place of healing.

As my time in Tallahassee was coming to an end, my mom recommended a new primary care doctor for me. A few years earlier, I had stopped taking Zoloft because, having been on it for years, I began to feel it controlling my emotions and making me unrealistically happy. It was a weird and scary sensation. I wanted to go back on birth control, as my depression got worse around my cycle. But I had been too afraid to see a doctor to prescribe it.

Dr. Kay was my mom's doctor and went to our hometown church. I was so nervous and scared to see her. I told Dr. Kay about my past and what I wanted to do medication-wise. She listened, and her tone and body language weren't judgmental. All the emotions hit me while telling my story, and I started to cry. I cried because she heard me, she saw me, and she didn't judge my scars. She gave me the prescription for birth control and restored my trust in medical professionals. She has been my primary care doctor ever since.

I made great progress that month and the months after. I was able to see doctors again and take care of my health. I also started to get acupuncture for chronic neck and shoulder pain, an unexplainable pain I'd had since childhood. I had dozens of sessions with my acupuncturist and had become really comfortable with the process. But one day, something went wrong.

As I lay there, she put the needles in like normal. But this time she put a few in my left arm—not near my scars, just on the same arm. As she inserted them, I had a flashback to the needle they used to numb my arm right before they put the stitches in at the ER.

She finished putting in the acupuncture needles and left the room for forty-five minutes as she normally did. But this time, I felt paralyzed. I knew I could hit the emergency button and she would come back in and take the needles out. But I couldn't move; I couldn't think. The acupuncture needles felt like knives. They burned and froze me.

For the next forty-five minutes, I went back five years in time. I was back in that tiny emergency room getting stitches. I felt the pain; I smelled the medical scent of the room; I heard the nurse tell me to sit still while the doctor worked. I tasted my salty tears because the pain was so great. I felt the pain, but I also felt the numbness and the sensation of my arm being stitched with needle and thread. I felt the pull and tug. I had the same sick feeling in the pit of my stomach.

Finally, my acupuncturist came back into the room and removed the needles like normal. I kept myself together long enough to pay and get to my car. Then I broke down. I ugly cried all the way home. I had never had a flashback that bad, that real. I was afraid to go back, worried it would happen again.

Having worked through my PTSD does not mean it's gone from my life. Dr. Jill told me it would stay with me and I might still have flashbacks. But by working on it, the memories would not haunt me, and the flashbacks would not completely shut down my world. I would recognize the feelings and work through them.

Dr. Jill was right. The next week I did go back, and I summoned up the courage to tell my acupuncturist what happened. I told her about the seventy-four hours. She was so understanding and kind to me. She never put needles in my left arm again, and I never experienced a flashback in an acupuncture session again.

CHAPTER TEN

Dear God

One thing I still had not fully addressed in my recovery with Dr. Jill was why I use NSSI as a coping strategy. Because of this, six years after being released from Nicole's Place and a year after working on my PTSD, the thoughts were still there. They were always there when I was upset, sad, or just doing normal, everyday things. When I needed any solution or resolution, my thoughts would still turn to self-injury.

When self-injury didn't work, I just escaped my life. One of my favorite pastimes was watching a good movie or TV show. I had a great collection of my favorites on DVD and would pop one into the player when I needed an escape. As technology changed, my DVDs turned into digital copies living on my hard drive. Then the world of streaming came along and binge-watching TV shows became a new world for me. Streaming made it so easy to escape for unknown hours into countless shows I would have never seen before.

As I did my normal Netflix search one day, I came across *Felicity*. When it was originally on TV, I had seen maybe one episode but that's it because the show hadn't interested me. But now as an adult who had graduated from college, it seemed like an interesting show to watch and not too much of a commitment at four seasons. Over a long weekend, I watched it nonstop. During this super-binge, I even dreamed of the show when I slept; that's how I knew I had watched too much. But since I was really depressed, I couldn't stop myself.

Now, so many years later, I don't remember much about the show. I remember it was about college and that it brought me right back to my college days. It was triggering, and it frustrated me. It frustrated me because six years after my college days, I was still stuck in college. I hadn't grown past my unhealthy coping habits.

I have spent so long dealing with my PTSD; why is self-injury still such a part of me? I thought.

I had done therapy with Dr. Jill. I had talked to my family and friends about the hospital and what I had been going through.

Do I need more help? NO!

I was done. I was mad. I was mad at me? No. I was mad at God! I yelled and prayed to Him.

"I have done all this work! I was tortured in a mental hospital. I was treated like dirt. I went back for treatment and learned that I have PTSD, and I worked through that! I have done everything. I have tried to become healthy and whole, and still I deal with NSSI!"

I wasn't on my knees when I said this. I was flat on my face, lying on my bed with my head where my feet would be when I sleep. I was getting no godly answers through my angry and tearful prayer.

In the silence, I began a Google search for answers. I typed in, "Why do I struggle with self-injury?" Google brought me to pages about the disease. Then I saw it. I kept seeing it and couldn't stop. A common reason for coping with self-injury is having been "sexually abused."

I had read this many years before; it was always in the back of my head. I never told anyone, and I never let myself think about it too much. I just told myself that *that* did not happen to me, that I must be dealing with NSSI for other reasons. But that day, it struck me like a punch to the gut. It stayed there, and it's all I could think about.

Then the pain and tension went away. In that moment, I knew that sexual abuse had resulted in my NSSI. The room fell silent. I couldn't hear the cars driving outside my window. My brain emptied. My body lay flat on the bed. I felt like an empty vessel, all the junk filling my brain and my body pains were gone.

Just moments before, I had truly been at my lowest. I had done every human thing I knew to deal with my mental health, and still I had been at a loss. That's when I had come to God—

when I had nothing left. I had yelled at Him because I had nothing left to lose. I had yelled at Him because I, a human He had made, was made so flawed and He wouldn't tell me why.

Yet, now I was open to anything. I threw out my human fears, doubts, and speculations. I was open to whatever the truth might be. In that moment, my faith was the size of a mustard seed. Nothing was impossible. Then, God showed me my truth.

There was baby Stephanie in her crib, around two years old. My point of view was from a high angle, as if from a security camera. I saw a close family member—I'll call him Person C— walk into the room. His face was very clear to me. I knew it was him right away. He walked up to baby Stephanie and put his finger where it didn't belong—in a child or nonconsenting adult. Baby Stephanie was still asleep, and after this act, he left.

In a flash, the scene disappeared from my head. Then there was just silence. I was back in my head and I thought, *Was that real? Did that really happen to me? Am I seeing a memory? How could it be a memory with me so young? I wasn't even awake ...*

Then I heard a voice in my head, which I knew for sure was not mine. It was God's voice.

"That is your truth. This is the truth behind your NSSI."

In that moment, it all hit me. My life hit me. Everything became clear. I traced moments of my life, and it all clicked. Thoughts and feelings I never understood before all made sense with this puzzle piece in place.

For as long as I can remember, I had an obsession with Person C liking me. I wanted him to think I was "cool" and want to spend time with me. I never understood why. I didn't have these feelings toward other family members. Now, I saw that I was the victim of trauma; my brain had rewired itself, and I had sought approval from my abuser.

* * * * *

Almost two years before I learned my new truth, my mom and I were out of town staying with Person C. Since the musical *Wicked* came out, my favorite singer has been Idina Menzel. I'm a fan of everything she does; love her, love her voice, love it all! In 2010, I saw that she was going on tour and would be in Person C's town.

This was the first time I was old enough to drink with Person C, so he was excited to teach me to drink tequila. We had a couple of shots at his house, with my mom and Person C's husband (yes, Person C is gay) not partaking. We were just having our own little party—carefree and really careless. He had the bright idea to walk the streets at night. So, Person C filled us each a full cup of tequila and we were on our way.

My mom fought this, but he convinced her we were fine. Person C said, "Don't you trust me?"

Deep down, she did not, but she couldn't stop us from leaving. I should mention that I had never done a lot of drinking. But I was excited to be with Person C, and he was cool—so I wanted him to think I was cool too. I never drank when I was underage or got drunk with my friends, but all my common sense went out the window when I drank with him.

We were walking the streets, made a few stops, and then everything went blank. I don't remember anything else. The next thing I saw were police officers' feet. My head was on the concrete, and Person C was in my ear yelling at me to get up.

Still to this day, I can hear his voice right up to my ear, with force and anger: "Get up. Get up off the ground!"

I struggled to stand. It was so hard because I felt unbalanced and my legs didn't work. Then I heard Person C say to the officers, "She's my family. She's fine. We're headed home."

The officers left. I half-walked, half-held up, back to his condo. When we arrived, I collapsed in the middle of his floor on his rug. I threw up most of the night, and my mom looked after me. She later told me how scared she was and that she feared I might have alcohol poisoning.

The next day, I felt like death. I had never felt so weirdly sick before. I could hardly move. I felt so embarrassed that I drank too much, and sorry my mom had to take care of me. The whole day I couldn't do anything, but just lay on the couch.

Then it came time to go to the concert, and I didn't feel any better. But I got enough strength to get on the subway. When we got off at our stop, I ran to a trash can to throw up. Not a proud moment—not proud at all. The concert was great. Idina was charming as ever. But it was a rough day.

When I was fully sober and could process what had happened, it struck me as all so strange. I wanted Person C to like me, so I had drinks with him. He kept giving me drinks, so I thought he knew what enough would be for me. I trusted him to keep me safe and not let me drink too much, just as my friends had done for me in the past. But he didn't stop me.

That was the first time I realized Person C might not be a safe man.

And now, two years later, I was learning the truth of what happened to me when I was two years old. He didn't keep me safe at two, and he didn't keep me safe at twenty-four.

• • • • •

In the darkness of my bedroom, after life had become so much clearer to me, I spoke with God. This talk was like nothing else I had ever experienced. When I say "talk" I mean I could hear His words in my head and knew they were not my own. When I talked back, I formed the words in my head. It was not audible talking like with another human.

As He spoke, He sounded like me. He used words I use and talked on my level. I asked Him why. He told me that He speaks to me like this because it's the most comfortable way for me to understand. He didn't sound like a booming voice from above or use language like "thou" and "thee." He talked like a friend so I could understand every word. This was the first time I had experienced a conversation with God. I had never heard His voice this clear before.

I asked Him questions about my life—about where He was at certain points and about the future. I asked Him where He was when I cut my arm so many times.

"I was there. I was always there with you holding the scissors, making sure you didn't cut too deep. I cried with you when the pain was too much," God told me.

Growing up, I was always skeptical when church people would say they had talked to God. I had thought, *There is no way that's a thing! It has never happened to me, so it must not be real.*

Once it did happen to me, I knew that it was *very* real. Since that night, I have had conversations with God on many occasions. It's real and mind-blowing every time.

After the reveal of my truth, I had to tell someone. Through therapy, I had learned that I couldn't just leave things like this inside.

At the time, the closest person to me, both physically and emotionally, was my Apple coworker Jason. We lived in the same apartment complex and had developed a longtime friendship. I walked down to his door and knocked. We sat down on his floor, and I talked. I told him everything, and as I shared, all the emotions started to hit me. I started crying more and more as I tried hard to get the words out.

When I was finished, Jason was quiet. I could tell he cared deeply and believed everything I had said; he was just trying to find the right words. What he said next, I could have never imagined.

He told me about the sexual abuse that happened to him when he was around seven years old. He had let it drown from his brain when it happened. But when he was a teenager, his abuser came to him to apologize. His abuser, also a family member, was going through recovery and needed to make amends with Jason. Jason forgave him. My words brought all this back for Jason.

Jason told me about the event, his emotions, and his abuser. Like in my case, it was a man. We both were crying now, realizing this huge revelation bonded us even closer as friends. He ended by telling me he had never shared that with anyone else. He had kept it all locked inside.

I didn't want to lock my experience away. I had locked away Nicole's Place for too long, and it had too much power over me. I was not going to give my abuser any more power.

So, shortly afterward, I went to Tallahassee to tell my parents. They were very respectful and listened intently when I shared my truth. They both were trying to figure out the timeline, as they didn't remember Person C ever visiting me in Florida when I was a baby.

I didn't have all the answers, and I didn't need solid proof to know the truth. I could tell that my dad was trying really hard to not say the wrong thing. He had enough training to know you don't blame the victim and call them a liar. But to this day, I can't tell for sure what he really thinks or if he truly believes me. I just needed them to know—and I accomplished that.

The last step was confronting my abuser. I had many unanswered questions.

How will I react when I see him in person? Will he ever admit to me what he did? Can I forgive him without him saying sorry?

I didn't want to wait, and I didn't want to put much thought into it. So, I bought a plane ticket to see him.

I arrived and met him in the food area of a mall. I didn't accuse him of anything or bring up the past. We just talked for about two hours on various topics. I can't even remember most of them now.

At the time, I was twenty-six and working my first real job at Apple. He talked about himself in his twenties and how confusing and hard that time was for him. He told me of his first big job in 1985. He also told me about coming out to his friends and family in 1986—my birth year. As he talked, I started to do the math and realized he was the age I was now when he abused me. It was a chilling realization.

Ultimately, my goal for the meeting was to see how I would react when I saw him and if I could still be in the same room with him. I learned that I could, but times had changed. I was not seeking his approval anymore. I didn't see him as special anymore. I saw him as a sad, aging, and angry man.

The meeting was over, and that's the last time I saw him. I have not made any effort to see him, and he has done nothing to reach out to me. After all that, I have forgiven him—not for him, but for me. He has no control over my life anymore.

A few weeks later, I drove to Tallahassee and talked to Dr. Jill about all the realizations and actions I had taken. When I was finished, she told me that since our first session she had suspected that I had been abused.

This shocked me. How did she know? Why didn't she bring it up before?

She shared that many of my struggles signaled I had been sexually abused. She didn't know by who or at what age, but she had always suspected it. That was very interesting to me, and I was glad she hadn't said anything before. I believe the truth was revealed in the right way at the right time.

● ● ● ● ●

While I was in Tallahassee sharing with my parents, my mom had given me some old pictures for me to digitize and a VHS tape. She didn't know what was on it or where it came from.

Years prior, I had collected all our home movies and spent weeks converting them into digital files; so, it was strange that I had missed one. I took the tape back to Orlando, assuming it had gotten misplaced from all the other home movies.

When I began to transfer it, I saw some old, random footage from when my brother and I were young. I watched as it transferred in real time. Toward the middle of the tape, I couldn't believe what I saw. It was a one-and-a-half-minute clip from 1988.

In the clip, my mom is in the shot. This struck me as strange because she was usually behind the camera. I saw and heard my mom talking about the day. I saw my grandma setting the table. Then my mom said, "This is Person C—his first time here in a long time."

She says this as he walks into the frame. Then I saw me, walking like a two-year-old with short hair and a sundress on.

Mom said, "This is the first time Person C has seen Stephanie."

The clip ends with him giving me a drink of juice and asking if I want anymore. Apparently, I didn't and I walked away.

This was proof that Person C had, in fact, visited Florida when I was a baby. I already knew it was true. I didn't need the tape to prove it. But I sent it to my mom as she was skeptical he ever saw me in Florida. She was very surprised to see the clip. I think it helped her to process my truth that I had shared with her.

PART 3

Recovery

CHAPTER ELEVEN

Faith

E ven if you're not a fan of Apple, you know the name Steve Jobs. Steve was the CEO of Apple when I was hired in 2007, the year of the first iPhone. He changed the way we work, communicate, and use technology in so many ways. I felt honored to work for him, even in a small way.

When I became a Creative, I was sent to Cupertino, California, home to Apple's headquarters. It awed me. I saw huge, amazing buildings where the products I loved were designed.

And Steve was so close! As we went through training, we were told not to seek out Steve and not to react if we saw him.

I had no problem with these rules, but I was still vocal to my training group about how cool it would be to see Steve.

Then it happened! I was having lunch at Caffe Macs, the coolest and best food court I have ever dined in. The room seemed to get a little quiet. The friend I was talking to looked at me and said, "Don't turn around. Be cool." I knew it had to be Steve!

Now, I was cool, people. I really was. Slowly and casually, I looked over my shoulder and watched as the black turtlenecked Steve walked to his office with a colleague. They were just walking and talking casually to each other. My eyes stayed on him the whole time. I wondered what they could be talking about—a new product, a new update, maybe about what they'd had at lunch?

It was a big moment for me. I didn't need to talk to Steve. I didn't need to be right next to him. Being in his presence just that one time was enough. I do remember thinking, *Wow, he looks a lot thinner in person.* This was just two years before Steve passed away from cancer.

After he died, his biography by Walter Isaacson was released. I bought it on my iPad and read it cover to cover. By the middle of the book I thought, *Who is this crazy, arrogant man I'm reading about? Oh wait, it's Steve freakin' Jobs!*

I enjoyed learning his life story and understanding the man more than ever before. But how he created Apple—the ins and outs of his business—is not what stayed with me.

At the end of the book, he talked about his one regret. It wasn't the products he didn't release, and it wasn't leaving the company in the '90s and coming back. His biggest regret was not spending enough time with his family. The most successful man I've seen in my lifetime regretted that his kids did not know him. That stuck with me.

After reading the book, my definition of success changed. Success was no longer about working all the hours of the day or making all the money, but about spending time with my family.

Sometimes on my work breaks, I would walk around the mall and call my mom. In these calls, she told me about the many meals she, my dad, brother, sister-in-law, and nephew all shared together. I would hear of the weekends when they had just hung out, not doing much, but doing it together. I longed to be part of the nothing—and everything—they did together. The burden of being four hours away from my family started to take a toll.

My second nephew was set to be born right before Christmas 2012. I smiled nonstop when my store leader, Marco, gave me the time off to be in Tallahassee for the birth. But with all my planning, you really can't plan a natural birth and, of course, he was born a week late. He came into this world in the early morning of the day I needed to go back to Orlando. I saw him for about twenty minutes before I had to drive away. It pained me so much to leave him so soon.

When I wasn't with my two nephews, my heart felt like a Slinky—one part in Tallahassee and one in Orlando. When I was in Orlando, it constantly wanted to slink back to Tallahassee to be all in one piece. I felt whole in Tallahassee but not in Orlando.

Back at Apple after the birth, I did my job, but my heart was not into the daily grind anymore. I had reached the five-year mark working for Apple a few months before, and the job had started to feel stale. I needed to clear my head, so Jason suggested we go to one of my favorite places: the beach at night.

On the night of January 1, 2013, we headed to Cocoa Beach, about forty-five minutes away from our apartments. When we arrived, it was perfect. The surf was calm, and the air was crisp, cool, and peaceful. Jason walked a few paces behind me so I could walk alone on the wet sand.

As I walked, I talked to God about my life and where I was headed. I asked for His guidance and direction. There was darkness all around me; the only light coming from the bright moon was reflected in the water. It felt like God was walking with me, holding my hand down the beach. No longer walking on sand, it felt like we were walking on water together.

In that moment, I had no words. I just listened. My mind went blank, and I only heard His voice. He told me it was time to leave Apple and that I had done good, and enough, there.

It was time for me to leave my job; that much was clear. But God wouldn't tell me what job I was to take next. He made it clear that it would be revealed later. All I had to do was follow His path. God knew my concerns. He knew my hesitations without me expressing them.

After the walk, Jason and I got into the car, but I didn't tell him what had just happened. It was too intense and personal to say in that moment. With mustard seed faith, I scheduled time with my store leader, Marco, to tell him I would be leaving.

Over my years with Apple, Marco had been a great mentor to me. He had given me the month off to take care of my mental health, had helped me develop leadership skills, and encouraged me every chance he could. And over the summer, he had delivered some validating news.

Every year while I was at Apple, employees would receive a 2 to 5 percent raise based on achievements during the year. I had pretty much received a 3 percent raise each year. But in the summer of 2012, things had changed. Normally, my direct superior would give me the news about my raise. But that summer, Marco had wanted to meet with me instead.

In the meeting, he told me my performance had blown him away. He also told me I was the very first person who would learn about their raise, and that he wanted to share it with me personally because it was the highest in the store. After hearing that, I got a little nervous and excited about what he might say next.

He told me he had looked at my salary and the salary of others in my same position. Based on his review, he wanted to bring my pay up substantially. Then he gave me the news: I would be getting a 25 percent raise. Instantly, that number empowered me.

The raise spoke louder than words. It said, "You are doing a great job. You are noticed. You are valued."

Now, here I was, just a few months later, making more money than I ever had before, and I was preparing to quit a great job. It was a huge move, but with God's direction, I was determined to do it.

The day came to meet with Marco. I was so nervous. I took a fifteen-minute break right before the meeting to get myself together.

During my break, I checked the email on my phone and read a message from my mom. It said the Director of Technology Ministry position had just opened up at my hometown church. Mom didn't know the details, but she had talked to the pastor in charge. The pastor knew me from high school and I had interned with the former Director of Technology Ministry back then. Given my history, he was very interested in having me apply.

My heart pounded hard, then harder. This was it. This was the next step. I just knew it.

I put my phone away, went to meet with Marco, and I quit. I gave him a month's notice so I could finish up any projects and get the new Lead Creative set up for success. We set my last day in the store as February 1. Marco was very sad to see me go, and he did ask what he could do to make me stay. But he understood why I wanted to be closer to family and respected my decision.

As January progressed, I had two phone interviews for the Director of Technology Ministry position, but I never told the church I had already left my job. The interviews went really well, and I knew a few people on the hiring committee. My last day in the Apple store arrived, although I was to be paid my last official work check on February 9.

During the first week of February, I rented a moving truck and packed up my Orlando apartment. I had an in-person interview/campus visit for the director position in Tallahassee. I heard that the job had come down to me and a fifty-five-year-old man who had a load more experience than I did.

But that didn't stop me. Deep down, I knew the job was mine. I drove the moving truck to my parents' house and unloaded it. I planned on starting to look for a house in the next week as I had been wanting to own my own home for some time.

The next day, I headed to the church for my campus visit. I dined with staff members, had a short, informal interview with the hiring pastor, and—got the job on February 9! In that moment, the power of God was not lost on me—I realized that my last official day with Apple was the same day that Killearn United Methodist Church (Killearn) hired me.

My new job and new life began. I could see my family practically every day, and I did. I found the perfect three-bedroom and two-bath house. It was rough around the edges, but I could see its potential. I became a first-time homeowner in May 2013. Everything felt right; the pieces were falling into place.

CHAPTER TWELVE

Recovery 2.0

had seven years off and on of therapy with Dr. Jill. When I moved back to Tallahassee, I started to feel a pull, like I needed more. I felt like I needed Christian community recovery. So, I sought it from Celebrate Recovery (CR), a Christ-centered twelve-step recovery program. It's an international fellowship, but it has a very strong following at Killearn.

Back in high school, I produced videos for my church to show on Sunday mornings. The videos were typically about different church ministries and upcoming events. In 2003, the church wanted me to produce a video about a new program they were starting, the very same Celebrate Recovery that I was now planning to attend. In the video, three people shared their mini-testimonies. I can still clearly remember where we filmed and what they talked about. It was the first time I can remember people in church talking so openly and honestly about life struggles such as mental illness, alcoholism, and suicide attempts.

When I started working at Killearn, some of the ministry leaders set up lunches with me. One of those meetings was with Lori, a CR leader. During lunch, I asked questions about CR and what it offered. Lori enthusiastically shared information about it and mentioned she had tried to start a staff ladies' step study, but no one had been interested. I jumped in and said we should try to start one again.

A step study is an intense nine months of going through the twelve steps of CR. It's similar to Alcoholics Anonymous steps, but generic so participants can relate to any hurts, habits, or hang-ups, not just alcohol.

Once we advertised the group, we found a few staff ladies who were interested in joining us. This group was nothing like I had ever experienced. Everything that was said and discussed was completely confidential—a true safe space. We didn't discuss the group outside of it, so when I was working alongside the same ladies who were in my group, it never felt weird. We all respected each other and the journey we were each on.

One of the early steps is finding a sponsor, someone who has already completed a step study and is further along in their recovery. This person is dedicated to helping you in your recovery and getting you through the good and bad times. Having a sponsor is an important part of the process. Although you can move forward without one, it's one of the keys to a successful recovery while going through a step study. I knew I needed one, but the thought of asking someone terrified me.

Our step study leader told us that the best place to find a sponsor was at the Friday night CR small group. The three major components of Celebrate Recovery are large group meetings, small group meetings, and step studies. I already attended large group each week, mainly because it was my job to run tech for the service, but I had never attended a small group. Large group is where all attendees meet and sing worship songs. Someone also shares their personal testimony or gives a lesson on one of the twelve steps.

But small group was this mystical place to me. These groups are gender and issue specific. I didn't know exactly what they talked about or what would be required of me. It seemed like a very personal and intimate time. I was so nervous just to go to small group and then to be vulnerable and ask someone to be my sponsor—it was a lot!

But when I slowed down and thought about it, I knew who I wanted my sponsor to be. Only one person's face came to me whenever I thought about this. The only problem? I barely knew her.

A few weeks after I had started working at Killearn, a woman walked into my office. I should probably mention that for the first six months of my job, my desk was right next to a giant communal office printer. It was loud and since any computer could print to it, it would run at any time without warning. It was a challenge to get work done, and the worse part was when volunteers would come in and make copies at the printer.

They were doing nothing wrong, yet their constant copying was really distracting.

On one typical day, I was sitting at my desk and in walks this woman who was very happy to see someone in the "copy" room. She introduced herself as Melanee with two "ees" and had more energy and excitement in her voice than I had ever heard.

She enthusiastically told me she was a leader with CR and was very excited to meet and get to know me. I politely chatted with her for a few moments. Once she left the room, I tried to process the burst of energy that was Melanee! Her friendliness intimidated me, but it also intrigued me. I assumed I would not see her much afterward and moved on to finish my work.

Of course, that Friday at CR, I was on stage setting up mics and cables for band rehearsal when in walks Melanee. I watched as she sat behind the drum set. We got to talking again, and this time she intimidated me because she's a drummer! I had never met a female drummer before.

As a kid, I wanted to learn to play the drums and even had a practice pad, but I never got into it. That night, I heard her play. Her skill, excitement, and passion blew me away. I continued to see her off and on at CR.

Melanee's face was the one I kept seeing when I prayed about who my sponsor would be. Then one day I went to a small group for the first time, and guess who was leading the group that I picked that night? There are five small groups for women, and I picked the group for those who have been abused. I knew nothing about the group or leadership; I just knew that I related to the topic.

Melanee led the group wonderfully, and all my hesitation and nerves about small group went away. I wasn't required to do anything. I just introduced myself and listened. I heard stories I could relate to as the other women shared similar feelings and struggles.

At the end, Melanee asked anyone who wanted a sponsor to stay after our meeting. I and another woman remained. Melanee talked to us about how to ask someone to be our sponsor. It felt really strange going through the exercise because I really wanted *her* to fill that role. After the other woman left, it was just Melanee and me. Then, I got the courage to ask her if she would be my sponsor—and she said yes.

That was in 2013, and she is still my sponsor today. Yes, I refer to her as my "sponsor" to others. She is more than a friend and more than an accountability partner. She is someone who will drop anything if I need to just talk. She is someone who will make time in her life to let me share. She is someone who cares and encourages me to stay on the road of recovery. I know I'm heard when I spend time with her, and that's a powerful feeling for me.

CHAPTER THIRTEEN

Inventory

With my sponsor by my side, I moved forward in my step study. Each lesson has its own challenges and tough questions, but the main event is the "inventory." The CR fourth step is this: "We made a searching and fearless moral inventory of ourselves." For a lot of group members, this step is a make-or-break moment. It's so emotionally challenging that many people leave their step study at this point. I did not want to be that person. No one in my group wanted to be that person, so we all pushed through and completed it promptly.

It was very draining and yet cleansing to write my inventory. It involved me examining my life and writing down significant events that had affected me, such as what had happened to me as a baby. Most of the items on my list were things I knew about, but as I started prodding, new things came to light.

As far back as I can remember, I have hated sticky things. Stickers, tape, bandages—anything that can stick to one thing and then stick to something else. I'm okay if I'm the first person to touch it, but if I see something sticky on the ground or a kid puts something sticky on me, I'm not having it. I even cringe a little writing about it.

Well, I knew this was a little weird, so I dug deeper to see if I could find the root of this phobia. I prayed about finding the truth. And with mustard seed faith, again, God showed me the way.

The scene: I was five years old in the playroom at my grandparents' house. My brother and I were visiting for a few weeks without our parents. The playroom, really more of a building, was separate from my grandparents' house, and I was in there alone with two older boy family members who were six and eleven. My brother, who was nine, was not with me.

I continued to watch as God showed me what happened. The younger boy started poking fun at me while the older boy just stood and watched. The younger one started calling me names, pushing me around, and using me as his "plaything."

I fought back. I was a pretty strong little girl. I told him I was going to go tell Grandma he was being mean to me, but this only seemed to fuel his fire and he became more aggressive. He grabbed my whole body so I could not move my arms or legs. He pinned me to the ground with my back on the floor. I was screaming in panic, and he tried to shut me up.

He grabbed a dirty roll of duct tape from the ground and put a piece over my mouth. He seemed pleased with himself, but I was still in a desperate fight to get away. He taped my legs together to prevent me from running. Then he taped my arms together, pulling them behind my head and taping them to a piece of old exercise equipment.

He then sat on me, right below my torso so he could look right at my face. He had a look of pure evil, full of aggression and power. I was still struggling, and he was not satisfied. He slapped me a few times in the face, then he banged my head a few times against the floor. Then I was silent, and he was satisfied with his work.

Breathe. This is a lot to take in. This is me, thirty-two-year-old Steph writing on my computer. This is a lot to put on digital paper. I don't write it to blame; I write it for healing. This violent scene has been shown to me by the power of God. And I'm the first to question it. How is any of this possible? How could I not remember, but God can show it to me? I have spent days, months, and years wrestling with these questions.

But where does my peace and reassurance that this is the truth from God come from? Faith. My faith grew to the size of a mustard seed years before, and nothing is impossible when it comes to my Father. God is my one and only truthful Father.

Because of that, God also showed me what happened after I passed out.

As I lay unconscious, the younger boy did a few more things to me, then the older boy started to get a little nervous. He told the younger one to take the tape off and leave, as someone might come and see. My abuser begrudgingly removed the duct tape and left.

When I came to, I didn't know what had happened. I didn't know why I was in the playroom. I had gone there many times to get a grape soda from the big fridge. I assumed that was why I was there. So, after I regained consciousness, I got my soda and went back to the main house.

This event got buried. The trauma was too great for a five-year-old to process. It lived in my subconscious, coming out in my aversion to tape. Duct tape has always been particularly hard for me, and now I knew why.

When this new revelation was shown to me while writing my inventory, it was hard to digest. It was even harder to take than the truth from when I was a baby.

Sticky things have been such an issue for me for so long. After learning where this came from, I became extremely angry. The fact that this boy did such awful things to me, and an older boy just watched, infuriated me. It was pure evil. I spent a lot of time working through this one. This abuse from my family was the hardest part to accept on my inventory. Although I tried, I couldn't forgive them at that time.

After adding this trauma to my inventory, it reminded me of something more—something I had never shared with anyone because I never saw it as significant enough. But now it seems so important when paired with the above trauma.

I can still vividly remember all of this. I was about ten years old and at my grandparents' house again, but this time with my whole family. I was alone in one of the bedrooms, and the younger boy/abuser walked in and shut the door. At ten, I did not consciously remember what he had done to me five years prior in the playroom. All I knew was that I had strong negative feelings toward him that I didn't understand. When he walked in, I felt strange. I felt uncomfortable being alone with him, but I reassured myself that everything was okay since my whole family was right outside.

I don't remember the turn of events, but I do clearly remember that he pinned me to the ground and sat on my lower torso with his face looking down at mine. Then he slapped my face. As I struggled, he held my hands down. His face was filled with personal warped delight as he remained dominant. I didn't scream, but I told him to stop.

I didn't want to scream and have my parents see me in that position. I didn't want them to think I was silly for not wanting to play with the young boy. I also did not want everyone to think I was freaking out for no reason. I was a physically strong girl, so I thought I could handle him myself. It annoyed me when I couldn't get my control back—and then I was scared.

A few minutes later, someone walked in—the older boy. Now, I know him as the boy who watched my abuser attack me so many years before. He opened the door, laughed, and said, "You guys look busy." Then he left, closing the door behind him. I stared at the door for a few moments. I felt abandoned, alone, scared, discarded—like rubbish in a trash can.

Next, the abuser found more evil entertainment. He started bouncing on my torso, which forced me to fart. He got so much delight out of forcing me to make this noise. I was so ashamed and embarrassed. As a kid, farting in public was funny. It was something I had control over and could make light of. But this,

this was nothing I had control over. This boy forced my body to betray me. I just went numb.

Eventually, my abuser got bored and left. Alone on the bedroom floor, I felt shame. I felt taken advantage of and powerless. But at the same time, I saw myself as a strong girl who could take care of herself. Some of the shame came from not being strong enough to get him off of me. I was always able to hold my own when wrestling with my brother. But "wrestling" with this boy felt much different.

At ten years old, I knew what was inappropriate and what was not. I knew not to let people touch certain parts and do certain things. But I couldn't say for sure if the stuff this boy did was inappropriate.

He's family. I wrestle with my brother. Is that what this boy and I were doing? I didn't want to wrestle him and I told him no, but maybe I'm making a big deal out of nothing, I thought.

At the time, my ten-year-old brain could not process this kind of psychological trauma, and I didn't understand how to interpret my feelings. After he left, I went back to the living room with the rest of the family and acted as if nothing had happened. I didn't tell anyone about this event—until now as I write this book.

Looking back, it was 100 percent inappropriate. Even if it had been my own brother, it would have been inappropriate. I said no, and he didn't stop. I didn't want to play, and he wouldn't listen. He used his strength and power to physically dominate me to get what he wanted. He disrespected my body—used it against me—and disregarded my feelings completely. That was wrong.

What would I say to ten-year-old Stephanie, who didn't know what had happened to her when she was five? I would tell her:

"Everything, big and small, even things that seem silly and unimportant, need to be talked about. Tell a parent; tell a trusted adult. If they don't listen, tell another. We're only as sick as our secrets. You will learn that important lesson in seventeen years, during recovery.

"What happened to you was 100 percent not your fault. You are not responsible for those horrible events. You are strong, and strength comes in many forms. It takes a lot of strength and courage to talk about this, and I know you have that strength. You've been told not to talk to strangers and not let anyone touch your personal places. Well, this boy is not a stranger, and he 'technically' did not touch those places.

"Life is pretty simple at ten years old, and I wish it could have stayed that way for you. But everything is not black and white. What he did to you is physical and psychological trauma, and it's not okay. The overwhelming emotional scars will not go away until you start to talk about it. There is nothing to be embarrassed about. Go tell Mom. But if you don't do that today, that's alright. We will deal with it together in time." —Love, Thirty-two-year-old Steph

You might be wondering if I ever confronted this boy. No. As the victim, I don't need to be in the presence of his face ever again. You might be wondering if I forgave those boys. At the time of my inventory, I thought I had. But as I wrote about these events in this book, I realized I had not. More on that later ...

● ● ● ● ●

Much of my inventory was about the ugly stuff in life and examining my part, if any, in it and making amends where needed. But it was also about the positive side of life. I learned that it was just as important to list the good people in it.

This was more challenging than I thought it would be. When I think of the good, I tend to brush it off as *some good stuff happened but look at all this bad stuff!*

When I sat down and allowed myself to look at my life in this way, so many names came to mind. Megan, sweet Megan, my college roommate, showed me so much compassion when I needed it most. Daniel and Jason from Apple helped me learn to trust men. My nephews showed me what pure love looks like. The women who were there for me in middle school and high school and still in my life today—my Girl Scout ladies—helped me so much, as has my aunt, uncle, mom—and so many more.

I had spent so much of my life focused on the bad that I forgot to balance it out. Fortunately, my CR inventory helped me take a long look at the good.

When I neared the end of my step study, my leader said that in the last step a "miracle" happens. I know Jesus performed some crazy miracles, so I kind of thought I might be able to turn water into wine at the end of the study. Well, that didn't happen. But I did feel a huge sense of release, gratitude, and power. I felt in control and powerful, with my past no longer controlling my life.

So, what did I do with all of these new feelings? I started another step study. I waited a few months, then I co-led a study with my previous leader. We had another small group, and it was just as hard and emotional as the first time. But at the end of the second one, I had a huge realization "miracle" moment. It's going to sound so obvious and dull, but it was almost life-changing for me.

My miracle moment was realizing that recovery is never over. Life happens every day, meaning that I will always have emotional or painful stuff to deal with. I'll never be "fixed." The PTSD, self-injury, depression, and abuse will never be erased from my life. Like an alcoholic who is in recovery their whole life, I will also be in recovery my whole life. But day 300 looks way different than day one. My mental struggles do not control me. I recognize them faster and deal with them promptly.

CHAPTER FOURTEEN

Found

Growing up, Mom and I bought supplies for home improvement projects from a variety of stores. After unpleasant experiences at those stores, I asked Mom if we could go to Home Depot. We did go but not frequently. So, the few trips we made to Home Depot felt like Christmas to me. That store had everything and anything I needed to create.

So, when I bought my house in 2013, I made frequent trips to Home Depot for all my supplies. One day, as Mom helped me paint the room that would become my LEGO room, I clearly remember thinking, *How cool would it be if Home Depot paid us to paint my house?*

Then the thought disappeared; I didn't share it with anyone. It seemed silly and implausible to think that Home Depot would pay me to paint my house. How would that even happen?

Fast forward two and a half years. I convinced Mom to help me rescreen my back porch. I did some research, saw some poorly made YouTube videos on the subject, and thought it was something we could tackle together. We made our trip to Home Depot and found the screen, spline, and spline tool that we needed.

We didn't run into many complications. When we were about to finish, Mom said, "You should make a video about this."

I laughed and sarcastically said, "Yeah, right."

Then Mom continued, "You complained about not seeing any good YouTube videos on the subject, so you need to make one!"

I didn't say much, but I continued to think about it. The next day as we continued the project, Mom started taking video with my iPhone as I worked. We continued talking about making a video, and she even said we could call it *Mother Daughter Projects*.

At the time, my sister-in-law was pregnant with my niece, who was due in just two months. Ultimately, we decided that the do-it-yourself (DIY) video could be a cool thing to show her and my nephews one day—a project their Oma and Stephie had worked on together! So, we took more footage and recorded an intro and what-we-learned section—and *Mother Daughter Projects* (MDP) was born on March 28, 2015!

MDP started organically while I was working full time at Killearn. Over the next seven months, we slowly progressed with more videos, a website, and social media accounts. As we continued and became more dedicated, I started to think MDP might be more than a hobby.

● ● ● ● ●

After working for Killearn for two and a half years, I was ready to move on. I met with the head pastor and told him I would be leaving in two months. I wanted to give him time to find a replacement. During those two months, I looked into other jobs I might be qualified for in Tallahassee. But as I prayed and reflected on what was next in my life, *Mother Daughter Projects* was always in the back of my head. I kept thinking that maybe *that* could be my job.

But how is that a job? I wondered.

I knew some people made a living by blogging and being YouTubers, but I had no idea how to make it happen. It seemed scary, out of my comfort zone, and having to work for myself— no, thank you! But as God continued to put MDP on my heart, I slowly built the confidence to say it out loud: *I want to make MDP my full-time job and business!*

Mom was excited to launch MDP as a business. We honed in on what our focus should be, wrote a business plan, had a logo made, and became a full-fledged LLC. My last day with Killearn was November 1, 2015, and the next day was my first full day with MDP.

Two years later, and with close to a hundred DIY videos produced, Mom and I were painting the outside of my house.

MDP team photo

It was a yellow color I always wanted to cover but hadn't gotten around to yet.

A few months earlier, we had landed a year-long deal with Home Depot for a tool campaign! Home Depot also hired us for a painting campaign, which is how we found ourselves painting the outside of my house in two days!

As we were painting, an exciting flashback to the moment we were painting my LEGO room just four years earlier played in my mind. I remembered the thought that ran through my head that day: *How cool would it be if Home Depot paid us to paint my house?*

Wow. I never dreamed back then that it would become reality!

In high school, I had taken an externship class, where I got to work with a video production company a few hours a day. One day, the owner was chatting with me. He asked, "What's your hobby?"

I said, "Production, of course."

"No, that's your job. What's your hobby?" he replied.

I didn't have an answer for him. I loved production!

Why can't my hobby be my job? I thought.

At the time, I didn't sit and explore that question with him. But for years, I looked for a hobby that I loved just as much as production. His words continued to ring in my ears: "Creating video can't be your hobby *and* your job."

Now, almost four years in, I run my own company and work with the one and only Vicki, my awesome mom! Combining my teaching and tech knowledge from Apple, my hospitality and friendliness from Disney, and my ownership and list of responsibilities from Killearn, I co-founded *Mother Daughter Projects*.

Mom and I create DIY videos for homeowners. We focus on home maintenance, improvement, decor, and tech projects. Every day is new, exciting, challenging, and unexpected! I believe it was God's plan all along to make my hobby my job!

CHAPTER FIFTEEN

Beautiful Scars

When I learned I had been abused at five years old, I put it on my CR inventory and shared it with only my sponsor. I worked through it a little, but that was it. At that time, I did not fully forgive my abusers. While writing this book, I began to understand the connection of that event to what happened to me when I was ten years old. As I wrote and made these associations, the abuse took control of me again. I got angry, hurt, and depressed about what that boy had done to me.

At the same time, I started a new treatment for the chronic neck and shoulder pain I have had since childhood. The pain has become worse over the years, which is why I started treatment with acupuncture in 2011. I have had X-rays and MRIs—and traditional doctors have never found a reason for my pain. They have prescribed me pain medications, which would tell my brain I'm not in pain, even though the pain is there. I masked my depression with SSRI medication for years, but this didn't do anything to help me deal with the root of my depression. This is why I always refuse the pain meds.

For my chronic pain, I continue to seek nontraditional treatment including acupuncture, physical therapy, massage, and chiropractors. The medical professionals I seek treatment from can *feel* the pain and tension that should not be there. The pain lessens with treatment, but it never goes away. My current chiropractor now believes it could have been caused by the physical abuse I suffered when I was five.

My writing, physical pain, and new connections all led me to seek treatment from Dr. Jill again in the summer of 2018. She helped me focus on me and get my emotions in order. During this time, I had to put the writing of this book aside. Through weekly sessions with Dr. Jill, meeting with my sponsor, and praying, I was able to forgive my abusers fully. I wrote angry letters to both boys about the evil they did to me— and I burned the paper. I watched both letters burn all the way. Once I forgave them, I felt a weight lift. I felt freedom I had not felt since I forgave Person C. Once this happened, I was able to get back to this book.

Forgiveness is for me. Sure, you could even say it's selfish. But really, it's self-preserving and the path to freedom. Forgiving those boys means they have no power over or connection to me anymore. I will never forget what happened, and I still have flashbacks and hard moments—but I can get through them now with my healthy coping skills.

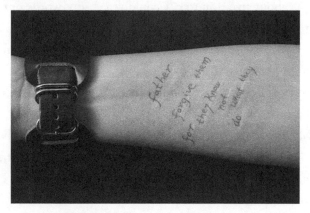

My favorite verse, Luke 23:34, with my beautiful scars, photo by Daniel Kuykendall

• • • • •

I don't live in fear of flashbacks anymore, though they still happen. One day when I was thirty, after we finished building and installing a sliding door at Mom's house, I started shaking. I couldn't control it. My parents and I were concerned about my physical state. Finally, Mom said I should go to the ER to have some tests run. I agreed, and she went to get her purse. My dad was sitting next to me and helped me stand up.

At that moment, I looked over at my shoes. I saw the pair of flip-flops I had worn over to their house that afternoon. Instantly, I tensed up. My head started spinning, and I started crying and couldn't breathe. My dad thought I was scared at what was happening to my body. He tried to calm me down.

"It's going to be okay," he said. "The doctors will figure out what's wrong."

For about five minutes, I couldn't get any words out. My mom walked back into the room and was dumbfounded as to what had just happened to make me so emotional. I finally caught my breath and shook my head.

"No, I'm not upset about that," I said. "I just had a flashback."

My psychologist dad sat there stunned with no words. My mom asked if I still wanted to go to the ER. I said yes. She got me in the car, while my dad stayed home. On the drive, I told her what happened.

"When I looked at my flip-flops, I had a flashback to the night I was sent to CRC. When I left my dorm room, I just put on a pair of flip-flops. I didn't know where I was going or how long I was going to be gone. As you know, they kept me four days, and my clothing was all wrong for that journey. So tonight, when I looked at my flip-flops, I was transported back to all that—in an instant. But the fact that I'm in this car with you right now, wearing my flip-flops, heading to the ER, shows me that my past does not control me anymore."

If you were wondering what happened at the ER, the answer is nothing. It was overcrowded, so a doctor never saw me. As the hours passed, I started to feel less shaky, so Mom and I went home. I followed up with my primary care doctor the next day.

• • • • •

I haven't mentioned romantic relationships in this book because there's not much to tell. I have dated a few men but have never had a long "close to marriage" relationship. I've had a lot of work to do on me before I could be healthy for another.

Even so, I do have a love story to tell. It's not the story told in romantic comedies—although I do love a good rom-com. My love story started at six years old when I accepted Christ into my life. He has been with me every step of the way. He has encouraged me, He has cried with me, and His unconditional and pure love has made me who I am today. I'm just a girl standing in front of her God, thanking Him for loving her well.

My Father loves me well by helping me see beauty where others may not. Scars have always been interesting to me. They make us different from one another, and they tell a story. I have many scars, with only one of my choosing.

One of my oldest scars is on the middle of my right knee. When I was about seven, I was playing with my favorite childhood toy, Omagles, a building toy with PVC pipe-like material. I made a car out of it, and my friend pushed me down the driveway in it. As I approached where the concrete slabs met, with one being slightly higher than the other, the wheel stopped on the bump and I kept going. My knee skidded on the pavement.

For a while, the large discolored scar bothered me, but I love it now. When I look at it, I don't remember the pain of the fall; I remember the fun of my childhood. I see beauty in my scars when I take a deeper look.

When I was twenty-seven, I got a tattoo. I see it as a scar of my choice. I can clearly remember wanting a tattoo since middle school. I always knew it would be a worn, wooden cross on my left ankle. I wanted that tattooed there because I felt like it was there already. Under my skin, under all the human junk in my life—Christ is here. He has always been here for me. The tattoo is a visual that reminds me of the love God has for me and my body.

I had a little hesitation before I got my "ripped skin" tattoo, which gives the appearance of a wooden cross emerging from ripped skin. I feared I might have a flashback to the seventy-four hours—or worse, that I might like the feeling of the needle. But when it touched my skin, all that went away. I knew it would be painful, but I didn't expect the pain to be so bad that I would want to leave every time the needle touched my skin. My brain kept telling me to leave—to get away from the pain. But I had to keep reminding myself that it was only for a short time, and the end product would be worth it.

As I sit here writing this book, I have to say that the process reminds me of getting my tattoo. Writing these words is still painful for me. Many times, my brain tries to convince me to not keep writing. But write I must. My heart tells me that I must push through the pain, because I know this story needs to get out of me.

Before I learned of my childhood abuse, when I looked at the seven scars on my left forearm they told a story of anger, confusion, frustration, and sadness. They reminded me of the trauma from the seventy-four hours and the aftermath. But after I began treatment for PTSD, I saw them as a symbol for how far I've come.

Now, twelve years after the scars appeared, I have discovered the abuse that led to my coping with NSSI. In my scars, I see the horrors that were done to me as a two-, five-, and ten-year-old. In my scars, I see the deep pain and internal turmoil the abuse caused me. And in my scars, I see hope. I see strength, forgiveness, and faith. The clarity I have now and internal work I have done is all there in my scars. What stories do your scars tell? Are you willing to hear them?

Five-year-old Stephanie

Conclusion

Throughout this book, I have talked about many of the mental illnesses that I live with and work through on a daily basis, one of them being nonsuicidal self-injury (NSSI).

Every mental disorder is defined in a book called the *DSM* (*Diagnostic and Statistical Manual of Mental Disorders*). The *DSM-4* was the standard for diagnosis for American psychologists in 2006. Back then, NSSI was known as simply "self-injury," or "self-harm," and was not as detailed as it is today. NSSI first appeared in the *DSM-5*, which was released in 2013. NSSI is the most accurate diagnosis for my coping method and is why I refer to it as such throughout the book, although before the *DSM-5*, I just called it "self-injury."

NSSI is a major part of my story. It's very personal and private to me, mostly because it's so hard for others to understand, unless they have directly struggled with it. NSSI is a coping technique. Unhealthy, yes, indeed. It can lead to a loss of blood, scars can get infected, and you never know how deep it might go.

Besides all the recovery work I have done, I have replaced my unhealthy coping methods with healthy ones. I have a "healthy tool kit" now. When I'm depressed or in a low place

- I write.
- I talk to my sponsor or a friend.
- I take a walk (my favorite being a hike in the woods).
- I build a LEGO set.
- I create art.
- I complete a small house project.

I turn to all or some of these now. NSSI is still in the back of my mind, where many addictions or compulsions stay, but it does not have the weight it once did.

Recovery is not a moment in time, it is *all* the time. It is every day that I'm alive. Life keeps moving forward, and I continue to work through ever-emerging struggles and emotions. If 2006 was the start of Recovery 1.0 for me and 2013, when I started CR, was Recovery 2.0, then this book is Recovery 3.0.

While writing *Discovering My Scars*, I discovered the importance of working *on* me. I am important. ME. I am worth spending time on and getting to know. Because my goal all along was to share my story with the public, it has forced me to write, and rewrite, my truth multiple times.

This journey of deep introspection has allowed me to spend a lot of time working on my mental health. It has forced me to take a deeper look than ever before at myself and has helped me heal in ways I am only beginning to understand. Spending time on me has been key to my recovery. And to you, thank you for reading, and thanks for letting me share.

Acknowledgements

I will not be able to thank all those who have impacted my life and my story, but here are just a few:

Megan, my sweet college roommate. You showed me compassion, understanding, and love when I needed it the most. We lost you in 2015 to cancer. I pray my words honor your memory and show your beautiful heart. I know I am just one of the thousands of lives you positively impacted. The world is a little dimmer without you in it.

Lauren, Renee, Marie, Mer, Megan, Emily—my Girl Scout troop. I love you, ladies! You have always brought joy to my life and continue to do so.

Mrs. Zimmer, my fifth-grade teacher. When I think of the perfect teacher, I always think of you. The impact you made on my life is still with me today.

Matthew West, singer-songwriter. I don't know you personally, but your album *The Story Of Your Life* was the soundtrack to my writing. It motivated and pushed me when I needed it most. Thank you!

Karen, Morgan James Publishing Associate Publisher. Thanks for believing in my story and for giving me much-needed encouragement to keep exploring and writing—and for getting my book published!

Angie, my book editor. Thanks for the editing guidance I needed in order to finish my story well. Your suggestions helped me restructure my book and made it more powerful.

To those already mentioned in the book: Matt, Jason, my nephews and niece, my sponsor, my CR step study ladies, and Dr. Jill—thank you for your unfailing support. I couldn't have done this without you!

Daniel, my friend and creative inspiration. From day one of writing, I dreamed of you taking the front cover photo. You instantly said "yes," which allowed me to put aside my self-doubt and give you creative freedom. Thank you for providing so many visuals for my book—especially for giving my heart the ease it needed through your enthusiasm and passion.

Mac, my retired greyhound. You came into my life when I needed it the most and helped me with the final edit of my book. You have disrupted my life in the most beautiful way.

Vicki, my Mom. You are my everything and have always been more than a friend. I am so blessed to call you Mom and work with you every day. #MotherDaughterProjects

God, thank You for loving me well.

About the Author

Stephanie Kostopoulos has spent over twelve years "Discovering Her Scars" through one-on-one therapy with a professional psychologist. The insights and experience she gained, along with her years in a Christ-centered 12-step program, shines through in her writing. Her authentic first-person voice shows a clear, compelling, and inspiring journey of recovery.

Stephanie lives in Tallahassee, Florida, with her retired greyhound, Mac. She is aunt to three amazing nephews and niece. She co-founded *Mother Daughter Projects*, where she and her mom produce DIY videos for homeowners as full-time online content creators. They were finalists in the national TV show *Home & Family's DIY Star* contest. They are sponsored by multiple DIY companies, the largest being The Home Depot.

Discovering My Scars details the first thirty-two years of Stephanie's life. As her thirty-third year of life began, she felt led to continue the journey by being an ongoing positive voice for mental health and recovery. Stephanie hosts the *Discovering Our Scars* podcast with friend and lawyer-turned-pastor, Beth Demme. In the podcast, Steph and Beth dig deeper into subjects presented in Stephanie's memoir, *Discovering My Scars*. They share "the rest of the story" not in the book—including chatting with guests appearing in *Discovering My Scars*.

While the podcast is inspired by Stephanie's book, the hosts expand on subjects that make each person unique. The mission of the podcast is to help people embrace the "embarrassing" parts of their lives and learn to love and value all of themselves. On the podcast, the hosts share their own experiences and invite guests to broaden the conversation by contributing their own wisdom. As in Stephanie's book, the podcast does not "tell you what to do," rather, it has the ability to inspire people through the hosts' honest and heartfelt approach.

For more details on Stephanie, please visit her at **StephanieKostopoulos.com**. Join her weekly email newsletter for all the latest updates.

Printed in the USA
CPSIA information can be obtained
at www.ICGtesting.com
JSHW082348140824
68134JS00020B/1957